Strategy

Strategy

A Guide to Policing the African American Community

DR. MAULIN CHRIS HERRING

ISBN-13: 9781530271344
ISBN-10: 1530271347
Library of Congress Control Number: 2016903690
CreateSpace Independent Publishing Platform
North Charleston, South Carolina

Dedication

This book is dedicated to those police chiefs and sheriffs who understood and demonstrated that engaging the Black community involved more than police-community relations, who did not wait until a critical incident occurred to engage the Black community, and who were committed to improving the quality of life in the communities they served, not retreating due to organizational resistance and backlash. This book is also dedicated to those citizens of the Black community who understood that in order to make their communities safer, they had to proactively collaborate with their local law enforcement agencies, committing time and effort to bring about needed change, not waiting until a critical incident occurred in the community to do so.

Contents

Introduction

I T IS RATHER hard to believe that my career in law enforcement started over thirty-four years ago in Chapel Hill, North Carolina, as a public safety officer (police, fire, and EMS) at the age of twenty. Over the past almost three and a half decades, I, like most in my profession, have experienced many trials, tribulations, and achievements. That time span has allowed me to experience covert narcotics operations, the start-up of the North Carolina Center for Community Policing, service as the first Black police chief of two communities, national consulting, and management of a national university homeland security institute. I have provided training and consulting in just about every state in the nation, as well as meeting with representatives of the Ugandan and Kenyan national police command staff on different occasions. During those early years, I served as a consultant and trainer for the International Association of Chiefs of Police, the

National Sherriff's Association, the US Department of Justice Office of Community-Oriented Policing, and regional community-policing institutes in addition to being an assessor for the Commission on Accreditation for Law Enforcement Agencies.

Back in 1981, who would have thought that a twenty-year-old police recruit who flunked out of the University of North Carolina at Chapel Hill would go on to earn master's degrees in public administration, sociology, human services, and divinity, as well as a doctorate of ministry degree? As a certified instructor for North Carolina Training and Standards and an adjunct and full-time college professor who has been affiliated with five colleges and universities, I have had the pleasure of instructing and teaching thousands in the field and in the classroom. For the past nine years, I have served as the executive director of the Institute for Homeland Security and Workforce Development and as a criminal justice faculty member in the criminal justice department at North Carolina Central University. Throughout my career, much has taken place that exemplifies the historic strained relationship between law enforcement and the African American community.

In May 1980 the riots of Liberty City (Miami), Florida, took place as the Black community took to the streets after the acquittal of four White police officers in the death of a Black man, Arthur McDuffie.

I had spent time working with my older brother in Miami around that period. In 1981 when I became a Chapel Hill public safety officer, the Black officers had a formal grievance against the police department for unfair practices based on race. Even during my early years in policing and before, many in Black communities throughout the country had a distrust of the police, and Black males were still disproportionately imprisoned when compared to other races. Due to riots resulting from police encounters with Black males, the following communities burned in addition to Liberty City:

1992	Los Angeles, California
1996	St. Petersburg, Florida
2001	Cincinnati, Ohio
2014	Ferguson, Missouri
2015	Baltimore, Maryland

My experiences growing up in Los Angeles, California, and my early career years allowed me to realize how disconnected many in law enforcement were from the extreme distrust and animosity that much of the Black community had toward the police and also allowed me to realize how many law enforcement officers had less-than-favorable thoughts about many low-income Black communities. My more than three decades of working with law enforcement

leadership and Black community leadership contin-
ues to confirm that the majority in law enforcement
do not understand the level of hate that many in the
Black community have toward law enforcement and
the criminal justice system.

This book is based on my professional, personal,
and academic experiences. I have been fortunate to
be trained by and work with the best community-
oriented policing (COP) trailblazers and during the
early years, including Ray Galvin and Jerry Needle
with the International Association of Chiefs of Police;
Deputy Chief Bill Smith of the San Bernardino,
California, Police Department; Phil Keith of the
Knoxville, Tennessee, Police Department; and Peter
Bellmio, a leading national consultant when it comes
to patrol deployment studies and strategic planning.
Pete introduced me to community-oriented policing
and crime-control plans, opening many doors for
my experience and success. These gentlemen were
the groundbreakers in strategic problem solving,
strategically engaging communities, and operation-
alizing COP as a management style.

Throughout the years, I consulted for, met with,
and trained hundreds of law enforcement managers, supervisors, and officers from large metropolitan cities to small rural departments. Along the way,
I came into contact with law enforcement managers
who had different ideas when it came to policing

the Black community. A few understood the level of distrust many in the Black community have toward law enforcement and the need to develop long-term strategies to strengthen relationships in order to control crime while improving quality of life. Some were clueless, and some simply couldn't care less. Among those who understood, some knew what it took but believed that they did not have support from their staff and local government management to develop and implement long-term strategic plans to address the historic problem.

Some of those law enforcement managers who understood the level of distrust had support but did not know how to address the issue. There were law enforcement managers who would claim that they had strong support in the Black community and everything was OK, while statistics and members of the Black community told a different story. There were those law enforcement managers who simply wanted to do their time as peacefully as possible until they reached retirement. There were those law enforcement executives who thought they had all of the answers and could handle everything their way, and some were eventually forced out of office due to high levels of crime and community dissatisfaction. There were those police chiefs and sheriffs who knew of a few racist officers and deputies but did not know how to address them or had no problem with them as long as they did not create problems. And there were those law enforcement managers who believed the Black community was the same as all other parts of the community and did not warrant any "special" attention.

I have also met African American community leaders with diverse beliefs about collaboration between the Black community and law enforcement. There were those self-proclaimed leaders who presented themselves as the voices of the entire Black community, and they were not. There were those self-serving leaders who were only interested in their own agendas. There were the political leaders who were only interested in keeping their elected positions. There were the angry leaders who had personal vendettas against law enforcement, were not patient, and for the most part, could not be satisfied, no matter what actions law enforcement took. There were the Black community leaders who would come out with anger and calls for change after a shooting or a critical incident and then go back behind closed doors once the media had little interest and once they realized the hard work and time commitment needed. And yes, there were those Black leaders who understood that something needed to be done but could not get the community and law enforcement to commit to long-term collaboration that would bring about the needed change.

So here we are with crime statistics not much better in the African American community than decades prior and in some cities worse, distrust among many in the Black community just as high or higher, Black male incarceration rates still disproportionate, videotapes exposing unjustified use of force, and riots still occurring. I am simply amazed at how law enforcement and the Black community cannot find common ground through long-term strategic planning that can put an end to the madness, improving quality of life and safety for all—because it exists.

Strategy: A Guide to Policing the African American Community is written for law enforcement leadership, community leaders, elected officials, and criminal justice students who can benefit from a basic guide to understanding African American community collaboration and an overview of what to consider when developing a long-term strategic plan on reducing crime, improving relationships, and improving quality of life for all citizens. All too often, many want a quick fix for problems that have been in the making for decades, if not centuries.

There are three primary categories that should be considered when preparing to strategically engage the African American community:

- organizational assessment and transformation
- African American community engagement
- whole-community crime reduction strategic planning

Strategy: A Guide to Policing the African American Community is divided into four chapters based on the concepts referenced above. Chapter 1, "Organizational Assessment and Transformation in Preparation for Minority Community Engagement," provides specific elements that a law enforcement organization should practice to prepare itself for successful minority community long-term engagement. Some of those topics include garnering support, hiring/recruiting, patrol deployment staffing, increasing case closure rates, implementing crime analysis, developing complaint tracking and early warning systems, training, and evaluating employees. Chapter 1 also provides a brief discussion on organizational backlash as a result of employee resistance.

Chapter 2, "Law Enforcement and Black Male Typologies," provides an overview of diverse typologies of law enforcement officers as well as an overview of the diversity of Black men. The law enforcement officer typologies allow law enforcement managers to reflect on those that may work in their organizations, needed policies, training, and protocol to address problem personalities, and support for those officers who can assist with engaging the Black community. This chapter also serves as reminder to community leaders that there are good, positive law enforcement officers who work in their communities. Just as many in the Black community often label all law enforcement as the same, many in law enforcement label all Black men as the same, not appreciating valuable resources and opportunities.

The discussion of the diversity of Black men is a great transition to chapter 3, "African American Community Engagement." This chapter provides a brief and selected list of organizations in the African American community that many law enforcement and local government managers may not be aware of and some in the Black community may take for granted. Engaging the Black community calls for collaborating with organizations to assist with implementing long-term strategies that improve quality of life, improve law enforcement relationships and reduce crime. Organizations discussed include public housing residential counsels, faith community leaders, masonic community leaders, historically Black colleges and universities (HBCUs), business community leaders, and fraternities and sororities.

The fourth and final chapter, "Whole-Community Crime-Reduction Strategic Planning and Community Engagement," addresses strategies and methods for whole-community crime-reduction strategic planning and community engagement. Chapter 4 provides an overview of the strategic planning elements, which include selecting the program manager, establishing an implementation committee, selecting the first communitywide strategy session date, marketing the strategy session, developing the agenda, hosting the strategy session, and following up with working group committees. Chapter 4 also lays out the methodology that will solicit a community's commitment.

Here is what is amazing. The unnecessary injuries to law enforcement officers and citizens; the riots; the historic, disproportionately high crime rates, including victimization in many Black communities; the disproportionate arrest rates; and the fear and anger can all absolutely be reduced and improved. If egos, distrust, and impatience are set aside for whole community quality of life improvement with emphasis on long-term strategic collaboration, communities and relationships can improve. *Strategy: A Guide to Policing the African American Community* can assist in bringing about that change.

1

Organizational Assessment and Transformation in Preparation for Minority Community Engagement

LARGE OR SMALL, many law enforcement managers do not take the time to conduct a comprehensive assessment of their organization in respect to collaborating with the African American community. While accreditation is beneficial and is an effective process, it primarily focuses on policy development and implementation and not on functional analysis and impact assessment. Long-term community engagement to control crime and improve quality of life through community partnerships can be rather comprehensive but extremely impactful. Organizational assessment and transformation are necessary for the following reasons:

- having an understanding of crime by type and location
- having an understanding of how officers spend their time
- having an understanding of investigation case-closure rates
- having the ability to analyze patrol staffing
- hiring, preparing, and evaluating staff for community engagement and problem solving
- providing an overview of the organization, crime analysis, staffing, patrol deployment, case closures, and calls-for-service allocation to the community

To be successful, officers and deputies must have time to meet with neighborhood residents in the areas they patrol, participate in formal problem solving, and be evaluated on and rewarded for their activities. Promotion assessment and decisions should include evaluation of community engagement and problem solving. Interaction with residents in the officers' patrol districts, including the business districts, allows for familiarity and relationship building beyond responding to calls for service. The amount of time proactively spent in communities may come in the form of performing foot patrol, performing directed patrol, hosting a neighborhood meeting, participating in an established neighborhood meeting, or presenting at a community organization meeting (this will be discussed more in the community engagement section). Many law enforcement managers will quickly argue that they do not have staff to proactively police at this level, yet what they are doing still has not often significantly reduced crime or strengthened minority community relationships. The organizational assessment is the first step in organizational transformation that will prepare managers to analyze staffing for efficiency and effectiveness, reallocate resources, appropriately request additional resources if needed, and engage the community, allowing employees to have the time while being evaluated on efforts and successes.

There are a number of ways this assessment can be implemented. One is to hire a consultant to manage the process. Hiring a consultant is probably the most efficient and effective way to comprehensively succeed, depending on the size of the organization. Another consideration is to seek the assistance of academic expertise if there are universities in the community that are accomplished in particular areas. The next best option is to put together a team to develop and implement a strategy, led by one or two employees within the law enforcement agency management team. Within many organizations, this would most likely include the police / law enforcement planner. Another possibility is to have the command staff collectively develop and implement the strategy. This should be coordinated by a deputy chief. For smaller organizations, the police chief will most likely lead the process, along with the many other hats she/he wears. Smaller agencies should also implement the assessment, understanding that some elements will be less complex. In some cases, external funding may be available to assist with the initiative. I have worked on a number of related projects that were funded by the federal government. Private organizations should be considered as sources for external funding as well.

Organizational Backlash

Not everyone within the law enforcement organization will be excited about the process, the outcome, and the ultimate goal of strategically partnering with the community, especially the Black community, to control crime and improve the quality of life. Sometime around 1995, when I was starting up the North Carolina Center for Community Policing, Harry Dolan was police chief of Lumberton, North Carolina. He went on to become police chief of Grand Rapids, Michigan, and retired as police chief for Raleigh, North Carolina. As I recall, Chief Dolan wrote a paper on organizational backlash when implementing community-oriented policing (COP). While I did not have a full respect for it then, I truly understood it later as a consultant for the Department of Justice Community-Oriented Policing Consortium and as a police chief. The premise was that some employees would not agree with COP and would even attempt to interfere with any progress. Traveling throughout the country providing training for the Community Policing Consortium, I found that it was not unusual to encounter law enforcement officers who did not believe in COP and expressed that their agency was only at the mandated training in exchange for receiving funding from the US government to put more officers on the streets. Some saliently opposed the efforts to implement COP, undermining efforts as much as possible.

In Hartsville, South Carolina, and Salisbury, North Carolina, I encountered resistance from some officers to implementing foot patrols and officers facilitating neighborhood meetings. This resistance even came at the command staff level. As police chief in Salisbury, North Carolina, I had an officer tell me that I was putting their lives at risk by mandating them to get out of the cars and patrol neighborhoods by foot for thirty to forty-five minutes. To show my commitment, I would often walk the streets in drug-challenged areas and even moved my family into public housing for about one year. And yes, there was the occasional fight, domestic disturbance, drug activity, and noise complaint. Residents would occasionally come to my door asking for assistance. In addition, I developed personal relationships with seniors and other residents. Many never thought they would live that close to a police officer, much less a police chief. No immediate threat ever came to my family. After we moved out, I would get occasional calls from some residents when they had a problem.

In Salisbury, when I implemented a citizen complaint tracking system and introduced it in the local paper, an officer said that I was more pro-community and encouraging complaints against officers. Some officers thought facilitating neighborhood meetings was soft on crime and not real police work. In response to promotion assessments that resulted in command staff and ranking officer demotions, I received accusations of age discrimination, race discrimination, and sexual harassment.

There were other underlying issues related to racism present as well, and resistance to change also came from forces external to the police departments. In Hartsville, a council member stated that the city was not ready for a Black police chief. He later became a supporter with some extra personal attention from me. In Salisbury, the city manager received letters protesting against the hiring of a Black police chief with one reference that someone Black should not supervise someone White.

While my personal examples came from smaller agencies, my national consulting and training experiences and academic research allowed me to understand similar experiences in large urban agencies and communities. The point is, at one time in many law enforcement organizations, some officers greatly resisted community-oriented policing, proactive community engagement, citizens participating on hiring and promotion boards, and the policy changes involved. In addition, not all elected officials and community members were excited about change and focusing on minority communities, including hiring minority leadership. There were also the issues of union concerns when it came to staffing and shift changes, as when I worked in Decatur, Illinois. These were some of the reasons some administrations elected not to adopt the needed managerial policies and practices that focused on strategically engaging minority communities. Police chiefs and sheriffs had to make sure they walked that extra fine line, knowing that some staff members and citizens were looking for opportunities to have them removed or make their jobs challenging. During the late 1990s and early in the first decade of the twenty-first century, there were several police chiefs who were forced out of office in response to organizational resistance while trying to implement the needed transformation.

Some of the law enforcement administrators who were forced to leave office demonstrated the apathy of some in the African American community in not understanding and aggressively supporting those administrators who proactively attempted to bring about change. This is also the reason that the next section, "Garnering Support," is included. I trust that some of the high levels of organizational and community resistance have been reduced in response to recent community unrest over aggressive police shootings and excessive force involving African Americans.

Organizational Assessment Elements

I will provide brief overviews of elements of organizational assessment in preparation for transformation that should be considered. The brief overviews are intended to be just that due to the complexity of some elements based on the size and mission of the organization. Some of these elements can be rather technical, relying on certain levels of management of information systems and crime-analysis expertise. The exercise itself is beneficial, identifying agency gaps and needs. Those organizational assessment elements in preparation for organizational transformation are as follows:

- garnering support
- hiring/recruitment
- patrol deployment staffing
- criminal investigation closure rates
- crime analysis
- calls-for-service analysis
- complaint tracking system
- early warning systems
- training
- employee evaluations
- patrol-level community engagement
- community collaboration initiatives

Garnering Support

It is imperative that appropriate support is gained from specific aspects of the community. This community- and life-changing initiative relies heavily on local law enforcement facilitation. If a community leader or organization is the initiator, buy-in from local law enforcement management is essential. That is the same if local- or county-government management is the initiator. And, of course, it is hoped for and best if the police chief or sheriff is the initiator. It may be easier for the sheriff to implement certain aspects of the process as the elected head of the Office of the Sheriff. As an example, by the nature of the Office of the Sheriff, garnering support from command staff and midlevel supervisors may not be as much of an issue since they often work "at will" with the elected sheriff. With the police chief or sheriff as the initiator, the key components of support that should be garnered are as follows:

- city/county managers
- elected officials
- law enforcement command staff
- law enforcement midlevel supervisors
- sworn and civilian line staff
- unions
- law enforcement fraternal orders
- African American community
- community leaders
- business community

While the term "garnering support" is used, in most cases that will only mean holding information sessions and select one-on-one meetings. It is important that the sheriff, police chief, community leader, or local government leader has a clear understanding of goals, objectives, benefits, potential obstacles, and potential costs. A well-structured white paper or very brief PowerPoint presentation is more appropriate than relying on open-ended conversations.

Hiring/Recruitment

Most law enforcement managers know that hiring and recruitment are some of the most challenging aspects of managing a law enforcement organization. There are the baseline issues of integrity, physical fitness, mental health, and intellectual aptitude. There are the often additional immediate concerns of retention and costs. For some communities, there is the challenge of hiring women and minority candidates. I cannot begin to count the number of times I have heard law enforcement managers state that they could not find "good" or qualified minority recruits to hire. I would often reply, "They are out there. Why do they not want to work for your agency?"

In preparation for African American community engagement, law enforcement must hire those who are interested in proactively engaging the Black community and, more importantly, do not hold concealed racist views or unknown aspects of fear. Specific measures that can be taken are as follows:

- recruit at historically Black colleges and universities (HBCUs)
- provide psychological exams that detect racist views

- include race related interview questions/ scenarios
- perform background investigations that inquire about racist beliefs

The recent public, aggressive, and deadly actions of some in law enforcement toward Black males have created another phenomenon: outstanding, educated Black males and females having second thoughts about joining local law enforcement agencies. As a professor at North Carolina Central University (NCCU) in the criminal justice department, I have had several students question whether they wanted to continue their journeys to become local law enforcement officers in response to the recent aggressive law enforcement actions and negative media coverage. Most professors remind them that they are what is needed in the field to foster change. HBCUs and minority-serving institutions serve as an excellent source to hire minority employees as well as White employees who earn degrees at these institutions.

HBCUs

There are numerous HBCUs and other historically minority-serving universities and colleges with criminal justice–related degrees. For example, NCCU offers a Bachelor of Science degree in criminal justice. The department averages more than six hundred undergraduate students and approximately fifty graduate students. The undergraduate program offers concentrations in law enforcement, homeland security, juvenile justice, and corrections. Students are mandated to complete community service hours and an internship. Graduates have gone on to work with numerous local, state, and federal law enforcement agencies, reaching supervisory ranks of all levels. As a graduate, the program prepared me well as I advanced throughout my career. NCCU is just one of many HBCUs and minority-serving universities and colleges with criminal justice–related programs. In addition, there are numerous other two-year and four-year degree programs that do an outstanding job of preparing students to engage minority and underserved communities. Many of these schools host career fairs and welcome classroom presentations. Law enforcement agencies with the greatest level of success engage universities and colleges at additional levels, including:

- serving on criminal justice program advisory boards
- offering internships
- encouraging student participation in community programs (ride-along, citizen police academies, etc.)
- offering workshops to students (physical agility, background investigation preparation, and the like)

Throughout my national travels spanning more than two decades of facilitating workshops and consulting, I have encountered many law enforcement executives who state that they recruit at HBCUs but have little success. After further discussion, I often find that their efforts are haphazard and limited.

Psychological Exams

While not a specific area of expertise for me, I do believe that psychological exams can play a role in assisting with hiring candidates that will benefit in strategically engaging the African American and other minority communities. When I was a Chapel Hill public safety officer in the early '80s, the department would use psychologists for certain employee issues. While chief in Salisbury, North Carolina, in the late '90s and early in the first decade of the twenty-first century, final-phase applicants spent time with a psychologist, and a report was generated. I was able to review the report and have staff follow up on any concerns prior to confirming a final decision. Many agencies at least have applicants complete the survey-style psychological assessment. The law enforcement agency should request that emphasis be placed on indicators that would identify attributes that may aid or hinder minority community engagement. Attributes and indicators that may hinder engagement include racism, sexism, reactive policing, distrust, aggressiveness, and anger. Attributes and indicators that may support engagement include compassion, cultural inclusion, critical thinking, problem solving, community service (volunteerism), and interpersonal communication skills.

Interview Questions/Scenarios

Different law enforcement agencies use various interviewing strategies throughout the hiring process. The questions are often basic or superficial at the early stages and become more in-depth in the final stages of the hiring process. Understandably, many agencies have become concerned with protected civil rights violations of applicants. I have three recommendations for this extremely important section.

First, law enforcement executives and local government administrators must become more serious about acknowledging and screening for hidden issues of racist thoughts that still exist among applicants. These hidden racist beliefs may also be expressed in the form of aggressiveness based on fear.

During an interview process, it is obvious to say that most applicants will not acknowledge that they have negative thoughts about African Americans or other minorities. I simply think many in law enforcement management have not taken the issue very seriously, maybe to the level that they take physical fitness, credit, mental health issues, or substance abuse. This is easily measured by the amount of time and resources committed during the interview and background phase. Related interview questions can begin early in the process and become more focused toward the end for final applicants. Psychologists, human resources, and attorneys should be included in the development of appropriate questions and scenarios.

Second, allow members of the community to participate in the hiring and promotion process. These community members may be able to bring insight into the final selection recommendations. Members of the local human relations council may serve as an excellent resource. Along with their insight and input, just having them participate will assist with strengthening public opinion about the hiring and promotion process.

Third, well-developed scenarios (written and live) can assist with the elements of emotional response during stressful situations. Many basic law enforcement training academies use these measures. Live scenarios provide some level of surprise. Once again, the process should be vetted through human resources. Many local law enforcement organizations have fallen victim to budget restrictions and the urgent need to fill vacant positions. Yet just one or two officers who could have been screened out can cause the organization significant cost, damaged community perception, and time expenditure down the line.

Background Investigations

Let's begin this section with a little exercise. Go on the Internet and search for "racist police texts, e-mails, and Facebook incidents." While this does not produce data from a scholarly research design, it has a similar immediate impact of reality. There are still a lot of law enforcement executives who do not choose to acknowledge the significance of the fact that there are law enforcement officers with racist thoughts and beliefs. Often the reality of research data of a similar fashion shows that the numbers and frequencies are higher than had been discovered. As an example, known cases of sexual abuse, spousal abuse, and homelessness are below actual instances because all are not reported. Often in criminology and criminal investigations, we will look at someone who has committed a horrific crime and then backtrack through his or her life to analyze the development to the point of the act. I recall attending executive officer training at the National Center for Missing and Exploited Children and reviewing an exercise on the anatomy of a juvenile delinquent murderer. We explored the different acts/signs throughout childhood that were missed opportunities for intervention by education, social work, juvenile court, and law enforcement professionals. Imagine if we had a series of case studies on law enforcement officers who committed known racist acts and could go back and see why their beliefs were not detected. During an online introductory sociology course that I used to teach, I would post a simple discussion question: Can someone have racist thoughts and not have racist actions?

More attention to issues of racist beliefs and thoughts can be explored during the background investigation phase. Many federal- and state-level law enforcement organizations often conduct a more thorough investigation in this area, and corresponding state agencies may serve as a model for local agencies. Asking relevant questions of the references provided by applicants as well as asking those references for additional references are just two basic examples. Background investigations in smaller and rural communities and with out-of-state applicants deserve a closer look but for different reasons.

In smaller communities, family members and familiarity with applicants may cause some background officers to not thoroughly and aggressively investigate some individuals. The culture of some communities may also make some investigators and administrators more accepting of potential prejudicial views and beliefs. Out-of-state applicants present the problem of cost related to thorough investigations, with most interviews/investigations taking place over the phone. Federal law enforcement organizations address this by contracting background investigators, who actually go to the home communities of the applicants, and using investigators from the US Office of Personnel Management. This, of course, creates a major hardship for local agencies that have to conduct background investigations of out-of-state applicants. One consideration is to begin working with local law enforcement agencies where out-of-state interviews need to take place. While I know this is easier said than done, it exemplifies the higher level of creativity that needs to begin for more thorough out-of-state background investigations.

Background investigators must be formally trained to ask appropriate follow-up questions to certain responses as well as have an understanding of how to recognize issues related to past conflict-resolution experiences. In this age of social media, it is rather easy to explore social media activity at various levels. During the recruitment, interview, and background investigation phases, staff can state department culture, policy, and practice when it comes to racist beliefs and acts. This is especially important for large urban law enforcement organizations where the sheriff and police chief are far removed from the hiring process. Those managers must define the culture of the organization at every opportunity.

Patrol Deployment Staffing

I will assume and trust that most law enforcement executives comprehend the significance of patrol deployment staffing. That is, they understand that the size and staffing of patrol districts should be based on geography, population, calls for service (by time of day), crime (by time of day), neighborhood type (business, residential, industrial, multifamily, etc.), traffic (including road type), and whether there are railroads or bridges. There was a time when law enforcement command staff did not truly analyze this information to determine district size and staffing.

Here is what many law enforcement administrators still do not comprehend and focus on: officers having time to proactively engage the community. In order for officers and deputies to attend community meetings, patrol by foot, and assist with formal neighborhood problem solving, they must have time to commit to these activities. Therefore, patrol deployment staffing should take officers' time into consideration. If officers are too busy "chasing" calls, they will not have time to proactively collaborate with the community. Before stating that it will take more officers or deputies, administration must take a closer look at beat designs, shifts, staff in offices, and what officers and deputies are actually doing. All of this takes access to data and an ability to perform the analysis. If the data is not available, that exposes another issue.

Criminal Investigation Closure Rates

Unfortunately, many Black communities are plagued with multiple types of crime that impede the quality of life and also often lead to law enforcement encounters, arrests, and victimization. Law enforcement managers must have a clear understanding of criminal investigation closure rates by type of closure, type of crime, and neighborhood. As an example, if a community has 50 percent unsolved homicides, and 50 percent of those are in one district, obviously more aggressive attention needs to take place, seeking assistance from community, state, and federal collaboration. The closure rate may be low for break-ins or sexual assaults. All of this information is relevant and must be identified and shared with the community to gain strategic assistance. Having a clear analysis of closure rates may also identify issues with training, staffing, case management, community relations, and technology.

Crime Analysis

Being the young man I am, I can recall the days of seeing the city map with colored pushpins all over it, designating where crimes had taken place. My, how far we have come. I also remember sitting on a rooftop in Chapel Hill, North Carolina, looking over a designated area to find the movements of a suspect who had been sexually assaulting young coeds. Based on data from previous assaults, the location and time span of the next assault had been predicted. While the officer I was working with was really getting into it, with the camouflage clothing, rooftop surveillance gear, and use of high-powered binoculars, at that point in my career, I only thought, "It's cold" and "How much longer is this going to last?" I was doing it for the extra pay. I later became a little more familiar with crime analysis in the late '80s as I worked the police planner for the Chapel Hill police department while fulfilling the requirements for an internship. The police planner had me working with Lotus 123 to use data to predict criminal activity.

I truly became familiar with the scope and benefits of crime analysis while serving as the support services manager for the police and fire departments in Decatur, Illinois, under the leadership of Peter Bellmio in the early '90s. I was surprised at the complexity and potential of statistical crime analysis in predicting and solving crimes. I recall attending a two-and-a-half-day course in which we were not allowed to use software programs or computers, only calculators. I created a crime analysis position in Hartsville, South Carolina, and strengthened capabilities in

Salisbury, North Carolina. Today, most metropolitan crime analysis units are large, well equipped with analysis software, and often staffed with civilians.

In order to develop long-term, measurable strategic plans for policing the Black community, law enforcement organizations must first have a clear understanding of all crimes based on type, suspect, victim, modus operandi, location, time of day, and so on. First, this information can greatly assist with not only solving crimes but also predicting where future incidents will take place. Second, appropriate information should be shared with those community members who agree to collaborate with law enforcement to control crime and improve the quality of life for the community. This strategic whole-community approach will be covered later in the chapter. Successful crime analysis calls for the ability to collect information and the software and staff to analyze the data. It also calls for patrol and investigations to understand crime analysis capabilities, utilize the data, and collaborate with crime analysis staff. A basic Internet search can reveal numerous crime analysis software programs and certificate programs. Law enforcement agencies must be able to analyze crime and frequently communicate the results with community leadership, not just rely on community members to access information provided on their department websites.

Calls-for-Service Analysis

Once again, it is imperative that law enforcement administration knows how officers and deputies are spending their time. It is not unusual for law enforcement managers to request more staff without first performing the appropriate analysis to see if there are other options. The primary goal in this case is to identify time that can be used to engage the community. Law enforcement supervisors know that the majority of a patrol unit's time is not spent on responding to crimes but rather to various types of calls for service. A very limited example of these calls for service may include funeral escorts, noise complaints, neighbor disputes, animals at large, parking issues, locked keys in cars, disabled vehicles, and the list can go on, depending on the community. Some agencies have found it more effective and efficient to develop civilian units that handle some of these calls for service, freeing up patrols' time. The questions are, what analysis went into the decision, how often is an evaluation done, and free up patrols' time for what? Due to liability, some agencies have decided to not perform certain functions like unlocking car doors and jump-starting batteries. I have worked with law enforcement agencies that focused on having citizens call in certain complaints and having an officer speak with them on the phone, rather than responding in person. The benefits are immediate response time and the freeing up of patrol officers' time. In many communities, a strategy to "sell" the option to citizens and businesses who want to see an officer must take place.

Residential and business alarm calls are in a unique category and call for specialized attention. Alarm calls must be handled and responded to as potential crimes in progress. Yet, in many communities, the majority of the alarm calls are false and often involve frequent business and resident offenders. As a police chief, I have managed the development of ordinances for alarm calls after analysis and determination that a large number of calls were false and made from repeat offenders. The ordinances focused on mandates for alarm company registration, business and resident registration, and fines after a certain number of false calls. Often, the number of false calls was reduced, freeing up officer patrol time with additional residual effects like reducing the potential of an officer anticipating that the call is going to be false. While not the intent, the ordinance sometimes resulted in a small revenue for the community. It must be stated that opposition from the businesses and residents sometimes occurred. This can be mitigated with the appropriate inclusive implementation process.

The analysis of alarm calls may focus on types of businesses or residents, time of day, location, and alarm companies. The analysis of all calls for service is similar, determining if there are particular calls for service on which patrols are spending a large portion of time and if that time spent may be reduced with certain measures. Once again, the purpose is to have a clear understanding of how patrols are spending their time and if there are areas where that time may be reduced, freeing up officers to spend more time in the community with strategic engagement and problem-solving initiatives.

Complaint Tracking System

My dissertation for my doctor of ministry degree focused on engaging the church to strengthen the relationship between Black men and the police. One element of the field experience involved a roundtable discussion with local law enforcement and members of a men's ministry. There were about six law enforcement officers present, representing three agencies, and approximately twenty-five men of varying ages. A deputy chief from the Durham, North Carolina, police department asked a question something to the effect of, "how many of you do not trust the police to police themselves?" There was strong laughter with side comments in response as several of those in attendance raised their hands. The deputy chief then stated that the police must do a better job of sharing that process with the public and provided a few comments about the process at the Durham Police Department.

Scholarly research well documents that the Black community distrusts law enforcement at a higher rate when compared to the White community. Many in the Black community feel that there is no need to complain about officers, and some may even have concerns about retribution. I recall writing an editorial in the paper while chief in Salisbury, North Carolina, encouraging the residents to make complaints against officers—using a newly implemented process—if they had any. I recall several officers becoming upset with me, murmuring that I was encouraging citizens to complain and that I was more "pro-community" than "pro-police." In my earlier book, *Destiny Fulfilled: A Black Man's Prevention and Survival Guide to Police Encounters,* I encourage Black men to respect the authority of the badge, even if they believe that the officer is acting inappropriately. I then advise them to make a formal complaint and seek assistance if needed. Often, if Black men feel that they are being treated wrongly, they will respond with anger and maybe even violence toward the officer. This is, of course, not good for the officer or the citizen.

A problem with many law enforcement organizations is that they do not have formal complaint tracking systems that mandate some type of follow-up with the citizen in a specified period of time. The complaint tracking system should be simple, identify points of progression throughout the law enforcement organization, include disposition, and be easily tracked. Everything should be in line with human resource and freedom-of-information policies. As an example, a citizen may come to the police department on a Tuesday morning to make a complaint about an officer who stopped him the previous night. The citizen would be informed of the process, and information would be taken. That complaint would be entered into a system and then forwarded to the shift supervisor or officer involved, with a copy going to the district commander. Hopefully the complaint is resolved at the shift supervisor level and is well documented, and the citizen has been involved or informed. In some cases, the incident may need to go to different levels such as internal affairs or command staff level. As one can see, I have not provided specifics or recommended programs, only the concept and general process. That all varies by community and organization. For instance, most police departments only have up to twenty officers with limited resources, yet a system needs to be implemented there just as much as in the agencies with five thousand officers.

Here is the issue: for decades, many in law enforcement and local government administration have truly underestimated the level of distrust and anger that many Black men have toward law enforcement, passing that hate down for generations. It has often resulted in community riots. A formal complaint tracking system is just one tool designed to communicate to the public that a formal process is in place, encouraging them to have confidence and reducing negative encounters in the streets. A complaint tracking system also allows for law enforcement administration to proactively self-identify any issues. The complaint tracking system provides an opportunity for law enforcement administration to include the data analysis in reports to the community. Some of the information may be used with formal early warning systems.

Early Warning Systems

While these are not new, many agencies are not familiar, comfortable, or confident enough with early warning systems (EWSs) to implement them and appropriately use the data and issues that they may identify. In an article published in *Police Chief Magazine* in February 2016, authors Frank Hughes and Lisa B. Andre state, "A growing number of researchers have indicated that approximately 10 percent of police officers can cause, or have caused, 90 percent of the problems in law enforcement agencies." Providing their definitions of early warning systems, the authors state that "an EWS is a police management database tool designed to identify officers whose behavior is problematic and to provide a form of intervention to correct that behavior."

There are several easily accessible definitions of and articles about early warning systems, along with a plethora of companies providing software programs easily found with an Internet search. It is extremely important not to "sell" early warning systems on the premise of identifying "problem" officers, instead "selling" them to the organization as a proactive prevention system that benefits officers and deputies by identifying behaviors prior to their becoming major disciplinary concerns, with the potential of saving careers. In addition, EWSs may bring more confidence to a community by its knowing that measures are in place to assist with high levels of customer service and integrity. Generic data from the system serves as an excellent tool to report the proactive efforts of the law enforcement organizations to the African American community. This organizational assessment should include an evaluation of the current early warning system or a determination of which system is most appropriate for the organization.

Training

One of the most critical elements of law enforcement and most public safety organizations (fire, emergency medical, emergency management, public health, and so on) is training. As the support services director for the city of Decatur, Illinois, I remember developing a system to categorize and prioritize training topics in the police and fire departments. The training-needs analysis began with surveying police and fire supervisors to determine mandated training, high-risk-related training, crime- and fire-prevention training, and customer service–related training. Most law enforcement managers have heard the expression "when budgets are cut, training is the first to go." While many law enforcement agencies have training units, not many have systematic, scheduled, training needs analysis programs with emphasis on evaluation. This is often due to budget restraints, but also at times the lack of this focus is simply based on administration knowledge and priority. Specific areas of training needs and evaluation related to the Black community are as follows:

- interpersonal communication skills and cultural diversity
- use of force
- problem solving

- conflict resolution
- proactive community engagement

With the exception of use of force, most of these topics are given little attention yet can have significant impact on reducing risk and liability. An organization's training emphasis often influences a young officer's perception of where the organization places value. Most agencies do not have any, or very limited, training hours focused on proactive community engagement. I would be willing to bet that very few states' training standards divisions include this topic in basic law enforcement training as well. Proactive community engagement training includes not only showing officers and deputies how to engage citizens throughout their entire shift but how to explain the benefits as well. These activities may mean simple acts like stopping the car and rolling down the window to say hello to young people walking down the street or children playing; getting out of the car at a basketball court for a few minutes to cheer on a game; checking out on foot in public housing areas; and walking into the neighborhood businesses and asking how things are going. As a police chief, on more than a couple of occasions, I recall pulling up to corners that were known for drug selling where guys were hanging out. I recall the surprise and nervousness of some as I asked how things were going and if they were doing the right thing. Someone, of course, always immediately started walking away as soon as they saw my car. Due to media coverage someone often recognized me as the police chief. I did this in comfort, knowing that my narcotics officers were working hard to make arrests. As a former narcotics officer, here is what I know: informants are sometimes gained through developing relationships.

There are the more structured and organized initiatives like attending and hosting community meetings. Law enforcement managers should assume that officers do not know how to do any of this and may even have fear or little interest when it comes to engaging minority communities. There is the issue of the new recruit, and then there is the issue of the veteran officer who has already been conditioned. One quick and easy litmus test that may bring insight is answering the following questions: What do field training officers teach about community engagement? To what extent does the field training officer discuss the use of force continuum in different situations experienced throughout field training experience?

I am sure the first things that may come to some officers and deputies minds are safety, time, and impact on evaluation when it comes to activities like foot patrols and neighborhood meetings. I am sure that the first thing that comes to an administration's mind is budget. In many communities that have experienced officer-involved shootings or critical incidents, the fiscal postincident cost to and reputation of the agency speaks for itself. This discussion also exemplifies the need for the patrol deployment and calls for service analysis that will expose opportunities of efficiency and effectiveness for proactive community engagement. Educating the public and elected leaders then opens the door for needed funding.

Training assessments should include an analysis of current training (frequency, cost, and effectiveness evaluation, if available) and training needs based on the following:

- employee surveys
- community surveys
- analysis of citizen complaints
- use-of-force reports
- pursuit reports
- vehicle collisions

While many agencies rely on quantitative survey methodologies, or use of forms with open-ended questions, there are other qualitative options that provide more depth of knowledge like small groups or focus groups. Local colleges and universities could be solicited to facilitate these round table discussions. Citizens may more openly share their thoughts, and that information could be analyzed into useful reports for the law enforcement agency. This qualitative method could also be beneficial for training needs assessment of sworn and civilian employees. Some law enforcement agencies may ask, does it take all that? The reality is, communities and organizations are more complex, calling for different measures. As an example, law enforcement agencies can no longer see diversity training as a needed evil that gets few training hours, often in response to a negative incident.

Interpersonal Communication Skills and Diversity

One of the most resisted areas of training in law enforcement has been cultural diversity. I combine interpersonal communication skills and diversity together because you can't discuss one without the other, although many try. It is resisted for a number of reasons, including curriculum developed by those not familiar with the law enforcement culture, a feeling among employees that it is "soft," and law enforcement often seeing it facilitated only in response to an incident of racism or sexism. In an attempt to make interpersonal communication skills more "tactical," there is a trend to offer programs that focus on reactive to and de-escalation of citizen encounters. This is another example of law enforcement agencies just not getting it, while spending a lot of money on expensive training programs to demonstrate that they are addressing the issue. Yes, it is extremely important for law enforcement officers to know how to de-escalate a situation once the citizen has become emotional or upset. It is even more beneficial for law enforcement officers to never allow the encounter to escalate by using their knowledge of those they are encountering, and this knowledge does not necessarily mean past experience.

For nearly a decade, during the '90s, I became known as a diversity training expert, facilitating workshops for law enforcement and other public sector organizations throughout the nation. Knowing that many White men in the public safety and public sectors were very resistant to diversity training and benefited very little from attending training due to closed minds, I developed a curriculum called "Interpersonal Communication Skills and Diversity." Following is the description of the curriculum:

> *Successful respect and understanding of diversity and the impacts on the community and in the organization are based on a thorough understanding of the interpersonal communication-skills process. Rather than primarily focusing on differences,*

this module challenges the professional to understand that individuals encode and decode based on several lifelong factors. If one understands why and how she/he and others think, she/he begins to understand actions that follow. This module was developed on the premise that you cannot teach someone how to act, ignore opinion, or respect others.

In addition, organizational missions and goals are discussed and the role the professional plays in delivering quality service while meeting goals is addressed. Professionals are reminded that there are numerous differences and that we group differences and commonalities for multiple reasons. Emphasis is placed on the organizational impact of individual action on the organization.

I believe that the curriculum was so successful because it began with discussing the benefits of improved interpersonal communication skills for law enforcement:

- reduced citizen complaints
- increased case closures
- reduced use of force
- reduced officer injury
- reduced civil claims
- improved community relations

The curriculum used light humor and practical analogies to address serious realities. Probably most importantly, it did not focus on pointing fingers and blaming. In addition to numerous law enforcement organizations that received the training via the North Carolina Center for Community Policing, a few select additional organizations that received this training included the Sioux City, Iowa Police Department; Phenix City, Alabama Police Department; Duke University Training and Development; Durham, North Carolina, Training and Development; the Washington, North Carolina, Police Department; the Knoxville, Tennessee, Police Department; the Knoxville, Tennessee, city government; the Clemson, South Carolina, Police Department; Durham, North Carolina, Technical Community College; the Conover, North Carolina, Police Department; the North Carolina Internal Affairs Investigators Association; and Orange County, North Carolina, 911.

I have often stated that state law enforcement training standards and local law enforcement agencies communicate the importance and priority of training topics by the frequency and amount of time provided for the topics. Use of firearms understandably accounts for the most training hours with mandated annual training and several hours dedicated to it at basic law enforcement academies. Yet those training topics that can mitigate the use of fire-arms—interpersonal communication skills, diversity, and conflict resolution—receive very limited attention. When I was a certified basic law enforcement instructor for the State of North Carolina, less than eight hours was dedicated to interpersonal communication skills and diversity. Funding and length of training is usually the excuse given for the limited hours. Yet, officers and deputies often ignite combative confrontations with the Black community simply by their interpersonal communication skills and approaches. This is often due to a sense of needing to take control and demonstrate authority and sometimes to a hidden fear among young White officers.

Local government administration must have a better understanding of the value of law enforcement training and support the financial costs related to staff relief factors. When it comes to diversity training, many companies have come up with an expensive curriculum that is simply not necessary and makes the training delivery limited to a few hours, rather than ongoing. When assessing the law enforcement agency in preparation for minority community engagement, significant attention must be given to the assessment of training. Just as much as law enforcement agencies send a message about what is important through the amount of time dedicated to training, they send a message about what is important through how employees are evaluated.

Employee Evaluations

While many law enforcement agencies articulate that they place value on community engagement, often their employee evaluation forms and processes do not support the claim. In preparation for engaging the community, law enforcement agencies must assess their employee evaluation policy, process, and emphasis. Law enforcement officers understandably focus their efforts on the categories that will aid them in getting raises and promotions. Many evaluation systems place emphasis on postincident measures like arrests, citations, and case closures as compared to proactive measures like community engagement and problem solving. Agencies must not only evaluate their evaluation process but their promotion process as well. Is there any—and how much—emphasis placed on foot patrol, facilitating and attending community meetings, facilitating problem-solving kits, and letters of accommodation? This is extremely important because it plays a significant role in setting the culture that law enforcement administration establishes. Of course there must be emphasis on quantitative measures of arrests, citations, and case closures as well as other evaluation variables. Specific attention must be given to patrol-level community engagement.

Patrol-Level Community Engagement

Many law enforcement agencies have failed when it comes to providing specific direction to patrol officers on how to engage the community at the local level and the value that comes along with it, as previously stated and emphasized over and over in this book. Most agree that the more time officers spend developing relationships with the residents in the neighborhood, the less likely it is that there are negative encounters during responses to calls for service and vehicle stops. This also goes for the business districts. It is rather simple: developing relationships saves lives, reduces complaints, and assists with solving crimes. Rookie officers will be molded into standards established by their field training officers, shift coworkers, and department practices. How much will they witness and experience community engagement activities and hear positive, rather than negative comments about the benefits?

It is absolutely false that it is different and more difficult to implement these measures in large urban cities. Metropolitan cities are divided into smaller beats. These smaller beats represent small communities. Measures that should be considered are mandating foot patrols, implementing directed patrols, attending community meetings, organizing community meetings, and getting involved in community volunteerism. While patrol-level community engagement focuses on individual officer activity, an evaluation of agency-wide community-collaborative initiatives is needed.

Community Collaboration Initiatives

In addition to assessing current patrol-level community engagement, every law enforcement organization must evaluate agency-wide engagement. If line officers are going to be held accountable, supervisor- and command-level staff must be held accountable and show commitment. Community-collaborative initiatives include city- or countywide strategies for engaging the community. Examples include the following:

- strategic communitywide planning sessions
- ride-along programs
- citizen police academies
- open sessions with command staff
- command-level community meetings with minority groups
- police athletic leagues

In Salisbury, North Carolina, I initiated round table meetings with Black men and police. I also initiated community engagement sessions with the very diverse Hispanic community. Strategic community-wide planning sessions are covered in more detail later in this book. Command staff cannot be too busy to be systematically involved in the communities that they serve.

Organizational assessment and transformation is important for any law enforcement organization and especially in preparation for strategic minority community engagement. It is not only OK but necessary to recognize that different communities call for different strategies in delivering the social goods guaranteed to all. Private industry has learned and has practiced the different strategies needed for their products, depending on the audience they seek to have as customers. On the public sector side, strategies to engage the richest neighborhoods in Beverly Hills, California, are different then the low income Black neighborhoods of Compton, California. Equality of service does not mean the same type and level of service, but rather what is needed for the specific community to improve the quality of life and crime control. As one can see from this chapter, organizational assessment and transformation in preparation for engaging the African American community is composed of many parts that work in a synergetic format with interrelating parts. It is important to develop a strategy of time frames, identifying needs and resources.

Before assessing the law enforcement organization, command staff must acknowledge the diversity among its employees. Some will be an asset, understanding the need or at least being open to the idea of engaging the Black community, and some will not be so favorable and even resist measures. As well, law enforcement command staff must acknowledge the diversity of African American men in their community and learn to leverage those who can support their efforts.

2

Law Enforcement and Black Male Typologies

WHILE I HAVE read a lot of scholarly articles that document the higher levels of distrust among the Black community toward law enforcement when compared to the White community and have experienced a lot of emotional distrust from the Black community as a law enforcement administrator, I must admit that experiencing the extreme level of distrust, anger, and even hatred toward law enforcement in the past couple of years even caught me off guard. Even when some Black males agree that not all police are bad, they greatly believe that the majority are. I was recently speaking to a pastor whom I highly respect, and he told me that he has spoken with a number of Black males who now have concealed-handgun permits, not for protection against robbers but rather against law enforcement officers that they fear of encountering. It has become very obvious that law enforcement managers and local-government elected officials have greatly underestimated the high levels of distrust, fear, and anger that many Black men and a growing number of women in the community have toward law enforcement.

In *Destiny Fulfilled: A Black Man's Prevention and Survival Guide to Police Encounters* (Herring, 2016), I provide a list and discussion about the different types of law enforcement officers that I have encountered throughout my career. Some I worked with, some I worked for, and some I supervised. It is imperative for Black men to accept that the majority of law enforcement officers are not bad, but even more important, that they are honest and there to help. One way of doing this is to provide an analysis of the diverse types of law enforcement officers; this will bring more insight, discussion, and reflection that are not based on emotion and public opinion. This analysis must show the good along with the bad.

When it comes to the organizational assessment that law enforcement managers must do in preparation for strategically engaging the African American community, they must seek a deeper understanding of who is working for them. If a law enforcement manager is not willing to admit that he or she has employees who have problems and pose risks to the integrity of the department, then there lies the first problem within the agency, even impacting national public opinion. That is a significant reality of today; local law enforcement problems and issues have national implications.

Law enforcement managers of large agencies must use their span of control within the hierarchical structure to make sure that ethical and integrity minority community engagement expectations are communicated to line supervisors and that information from line supervisors about line officers is communicated upward. If anyone feels that some organizations are just too large for this to take place, leadership must absolutely change. How can one fix what one does not know and is not willing to acknowledge? The question is, once command staff recognizes those officers that have aggressive or racist traits, the question then becomes, what is in place to provide them opportunity and resources to change perceptions or change careers? Supervisors, of course, may fit into these categories as well. In addition, supervisors must be able to identify officers who are eager to assist with implementing community engagement strategies. Here is an interesting point: over and over again, after reading these descriptions, numerous African American men and women, young and old, have said that they never thought about how diverse law enforcement officers are. This was even among nearly forty criminal justice students in an upper-level undergraduate law enforcement class that I was teaching, after they read the excerpt on police typologies from my book. They mostly thought about the negatives they often heard about, or the occasional negative encounters they experienced. As a reminder, these law enforcement typologies were written for Black men in an attempt to assist them with gaining a better understanding of local law enforcement officers they may encounter. The following descriptions are taken from *Destiny Fulfilled: A Black Man's Prevention and Survival Guide to Police Encounters* (Herring 2016, pp. 7–17).

Law Enforcement Typologies

I primarily focus on Black and White officers when referring to race, clearly understanding that there are many more races and ethnicities that make up law enforcement professionals. I focus on these two races because this book is based on my experiences. There will be many police types discussed that cross all racial, ethnic, and gender boundaries.

The two primary categories used as a framework for analysis in defining police types are Black and White. The next category is gender. The final two categories of officers are friend and foe. Let us begin with an example of those White officers who are friends of Black men. The first friend category is the Officer Bill type, named after one of my field training officers (FTOs). Officers who have just completed their basic training are assigned to an FTO for several weeks. The FTO is supposed to assist the rookie officer with connecting what was learned in basic training to department policy and reality on the streets. In most agencies, the FTO *should* be considered the cream of the crop, trained and certified. One must truly understand the impact that FTOs can have on new officers, especially those who are young and inexperienced. "Forget everything you learned in the academy. I will show you what real police work is," FTOs traditionally say to their rookie officers. And now back to the Officer Bill type, the White friend of the Black man.

Officer Bill

Officer Bill was the coolest White man I had ever met. This was probably because he grew up around Black people, if the story is true. He had an older brother who was also on the force—not quite as cool but very comfortable and genuine around Blacks. Officer Bill always had a coffee cup in his hand. He had bushy hair that he could have used an Afro pick to comb. One day while we were riding in the West End (our version of the hood), we saw a Black man walking. Officer Bill rolled down his window and shouted what some would consider racial epithets, followed by his famous goofy laugh. I, of course, was thinking, "What the heck?" The Black guy came over to the patrol car and started responding to Officer Bill in a similar manner, with negative racial comments. They both started laughing and shook hands, and Officer Bill introduced me as his new rookie.

When someone Black made a claim of racism against him, everyone who knew Officer Bill thought, "Yeah, right." Don't get me wrong. The actions that Officer Bill took were not always right; it was just that they were not based on race. This was exemplified one day when we responded to a disturbance at a biscuit breakfast place. Officer Bill had just started a fresh cup of hot coffee when we got the call. As we entered the establishment, there was a tall Black man in an imitation London Fog-style trench coat. The man was pretty big and loud, and he was making a fuss. He made several aggressive moves toward us and often placed his hands in his pockets. Officer Bill tried to get the guy to calm down, giving him commands and watching his hands. All the Black man did was get louder and more aggressive and he cussed more.

Being the rookie that I was, I started taking it all in while waiting to see what the next move would be. My heart was racing, but I was prepared to take action. Before I knew it, Officer Bill had had enough. Officer Bill, a small-framed guy, had picked up the large-framed man and taken him down to the ground—let us say with might. I thought, "Wow, I didn't know he had it in him." I assisted by putting on the handcuffs and picking the suspect up off the ground. All the way to the police station, the suspect shouted and made accusations of racial harassment and excessive force. These accusations were difficult for other officers to believe considering that the arresting officer was Officer Bill, with an assist from me.

One of Officer Bill's favorite places to eat was a little hole-in-the-wall in the West End that was known for soul food. His other favorite place was owned by a pair of brothers; one was his personal friend. The two brothers were of some other nationality and ethnicity, and they had light accents. Officer Bill invited me to spend off-duty time with him, usually at his side business, which was in rummage sales. His partner was Hispanic with strong ethnic features.

Occasionally, Officer Bill would even lend me money during difficult times. I developed a strong brotherly affection and respect for Officer Bill that lasted throughout my career in that community.

Officer Bill was not a company yes-man. He would let promotions pass him by before he would agree to conform. Officer Bill had his issues, but for the most part, he was a police friend of the Black man.

Every White officer you encounter is not dirty and out to get you. Although there are not enough, there are still some Officer Bills out there.

Officer Sista

Officer Sista is the Black female officer. She is usually a friend to Black men. As in other fields where sexism blocked the entry and professional advancement of women, in law enforcement, it took decades for Black female officers to realize opportunities. As usual, they had that double hit of racism and sexism. They were not only blocked by White males but also by Black males. Officer Sista is the best thing that ever happened to the Black man on the streets. While doing her job at the highest level, she understands the challenges facing the Black men she encounters on the job.

While fighting off the sexual advances of her White and Black male counterparts, she stays true to equality on the streets. She can arrest the most hardcore thug or murderer while understanding some of his deeper soul. She can do this because, to a Black man, she is a mother, a sister, a wife, a girlfriend, an auntie, a niece, a granddaughter, and a grandmother. She is the womb that carried him or is destined to carry him. Without question, she can do her job as a high-quality law enforcement officer, often understanding the Black man more than he understands himself.

Officer Brother

Officer Brother is the average Black male police officer—if there is such a thing. He can be older or younger. He understands the Black man on the streets at all levels. From the hustler, drug dealer, and just plain hard worker to the political, educated, or rich man, Officer Brother can relate. He is a true friend. If he can, he will give a Black man a break. *It is often the attitude of the Black man he encounters that will be the deciding factor (right or wrong).* He has absolutely no problem making the arrest or giving the citation. He is often struggling with law enforcement organizational politics and racism himself. He is more committed to the "blue line" than to the Black man on the street, but nowhere near the level of Officer Confused (discussed later). That is, if he has to make a choice among reporting something as excessive force, testifying against any other police officer, or keeping silent, he will often keep silent to the administration but sometimes speak about what was done wrong with his colleagues. If it is a serious racial infraction, he may report it and support investigation. He knows that ultimately he will have to depend on fellow officers for backup and assistance.

Officer Brother is a friend to the Black men whom he encounters on the streets, but some Black men on the street will present attitude, disrespect him, or underestimate him. *Officer Brother has no problem making the arrest, giving the citation, chasing, or using force.* If the Black man on the street keeps his cool and acts respectfully, even when in the wrong, he might get a break. This is yet another example of how the attitude of the Black man on the street sometimes dictates the outcome of the police encounter. A very important point is how the Black man on the street interprets Officer Brother's attitude on approach.

During a stop, Officer Brother most likely will be all about business, with his defense at an appropriate level until he has fully assessed the situation. The Black man on the street may interpret this as attitude, and Officer Brother's actions can quickly turn Officer Brother from friend to foe. Even if arrested or given a citation, the Black man on the street should keep a positive relationship with Officer Brother. It is fine to go to court and fight the charges, but understand that Officer Brother can still be a friend, and one can help the other. Officer Brother would rather have the Black man he encounters as a friend and future source of information, community support, and political support. As a young officer, I was Officer Brother.

Officer Confused

An interesting phenomenon has grown out of law enforcement in the United States: Officer Confused, the Black male version. This version is the Black male officer who has really been sold on the "I am blue before I am anything else" philosophy. He is very committed to the concept of the "thin blue line." He believes that it is not about Black and White; it is about being a law enforcement officer. He is committed to the brotherhood of law enforcement. I can understand how a young Black officer might initially go there, but staying in that frame of mind is another issue.

When I was a young officer, I remember providing protection for a Ku Klux Klan march. Believe it or not, this was in the early '80s. Even though I had a gun, a badge, a bulletproof vest, and the full authority of the state of North Carolina behind me, I had an eerie feeling when I saw the white robes and hoods marching down the street. In just a few minutes, I was called a nigger by someone White and an Uncle Tom by someone Black. It initially sold me on the point that a police officer was not Black or White but blue (the traditional color of police uniforms). The Black man called me Uncle Tom because I would not let him go past me to harass the Klan. I could see the anger toward me in the Black man's eyes. At that moment, I understood what some officers meant when they said, "You will discover that we (police) are blue, and your friends will change. We depend on and understand one another."

What is wrong with Officer Confused, who is first committed to the blue, the brotherhood of law enforcement? What happens when Officer Confused sees an illegal act, especially a racist one? What happens when Officer Confused hears the racist remark from his fellow brother in blue? Does Officer Confused speak up, go to his superior officer, and push the issue or speak to the offending officer? Officer Confused is usually blue *until the perceived racist action of his supervisors is directed at him.* Many Black officers have encountered racism from within the law enforcement organization. I say "perceived racist action" because there are times when the Black officer may be wrong in his or her actions or just not prepared. Now it is about race. It is at this time that Officer Confused chooses to become the Black officer who is in need of assistance.

Believe it or not, there are Black officers who do not like Black men. I have witnessed their negative retaliatory actions toward young Black men, although it goes much further. I have worked with Black male officers who could not stand anything that represented a streetwise young Black male: dreads, twists, baggy pants, nice cars, gold chains, and the like.

The first problem is that prejudging assumes that all young Black males who may possess some of these characteristics are thugs. I do acknowledge that some should be locked up until they understand that they cannot do as they like by violating others—as it should be with anyone. I also know that mentoring can eliminate criminal activity. While locked up, they should receive supportive efforts to aid in reentry into the community. Once out, they should receive support from the community.

I once worked with a Black officer who had problems with Black males seeking education. He used that as a reason to mark most young Black males in college who dressed—in his opinion—like thugs. I worked with another well-educated Black officer, and, as of today, I do not know why he had a problem with Black men he perceived as streetwise.

Officer Political

The next officer type is Officer Political, who might be Black or White. Officer Political is like some politicians—he blows with the wind or the power majority. He is more concerned with himself than anything else. If the wind of power is pro–Black man, Officer Political is pro–Black man. If the powerful majority's philosophy is to beware of the Black man, Officer Political subscribes to that philosophy. Officer Political tries to fit in with any group or clique in the community that serves the purpose of helping him meet his goals.

This type of officer was exemplified by a relatively young officer at the agency where I was a police chief. This officer was assigned to a special unit, which was a little unusual for an officer with his limited experience. He obtained it by being Officer Political. He was often in my office kissing up. He would give me compliments and would even inform me about what others within the department were saying about me—yes, he would snitch. The moment I left, he joined the not-so-pro–Black clan in celebrating my departure. During the pro–Black man season, he was a resource and benefit to the Black community. During other seasons, it depended on the direction the wind was blowing.

Officer White Political is probably more of an asset to the Black man. This officer's conscience will not allow him to go too far if political pressure comes from the community, elected officials, or external management. To save himself, Officer White Political will snitch on those doing wrong.

Officer Black Political is a foe to Black men because they automatically seek to trust him and assume that he is always in their corner. In reality, it is all about Officer Black Political. He has no commitment to the Black community.

Officer Klan

Officer Klan is the most dangerous officer for the Black male. At one time, Officer Klan had power and control in law enforcement and in the community. He would express his racist thoughts and carry out his actions in a lawful manner because the laws of the time allowed racism at the highest level. Even after the laws were off the books, he still acted on his racism because changing the laws did not change him or the public he represented. Slowly but surely, he learned that he had to be much more discreet. He had to figure out who on the job shared his views while openly expressing his frustration at home, maybe at dinner or over a beer. Like a chameleon, he learned to adapt. Some became educated and were promoted to positions of authority. The educated Officer Klans adapted to the changing times the best. Others were too lazy to seek education and could not be promoted, finding even more of a reason to let their internal hate fester.

One thing Officer Klan knows for sure is that he must be discreet. If the atmosphere in a department *does not* call for him to be discreet, real problems exist. When an opportunity arises for this officer on the street, he will express his hatred in the form of excessive force and manipulation of circumstances. But most challenging of all, he uses the legal police discretion to justify waging war against the Black man.

Police discretion is the subjective latitude that an officer rightfully has when enforcing the law and policy. An Officer Klan who gets promoted to a position of authority finds legitimate justification not to hire or promote a Black officer. He will find just enough justification to support the discipline of a Black officer that should have been overturned. This simple disciplinary action against the Black officer, just like the arrest of the Black man on the streets, limits future opportunity and promotion of the Black officer. Today, Officer Klan is real and ready to take advantage of any good opportunity. The greatest power a Black officer can give to a supervisor who is an Officer Klan is to cry racism in response to not being promoted or to being disciplined *if the Black officer was, in reality, incompetent and irresponsible.* While racism is real, clearly not all cries of racism are valid.

Officer Whatever

Officer Whatever is the officer who is primarily interested in retirement. He had high hopes and dreams when he first entered the profession. In some cases, in the early years, he tried unsuccessfully for promotion. If promoted, his advancement was limited. He has witnessed the focus on minorities and women and feels that he has been overlooked due to organizational interest in affirmative action. His standards are at the level where he will not play the political game to get promoted and will not kiss anyone's butt. Relatively quiet, he sits back and watches all of the different personality types and probably has the best understanding of all. When it comes to Black males on the street, Officer Whatever has no negative thoughts and really looks at Black men with a bit of cynicism. He may simply shake his head with a slight smirk. While he may cling to some racist beliefs, he will not usually act on them. He sees young Black males killing young Black males. He sees Black males violating and disrespecting Black women and quietly laughs. His primary goal is to work as little as possible and retire. He does take pride in what he does, however, and is committed to a small group of colleagues. At times, he may buck the system just for the heck of it. When there is major change or controversy, he says, "Whatever." To the Black man on the street, he is really no threat unless the Black man pisses him off. Then he is on a mission, targeting that specific Black man. Overall he is neither friend nor foe. Interaction with Officer Whatever is a great example of how a Black man's negative attitude can lead to an unnecessary outcome.

Officer Gung Ho

Officer Gung Ho is one of the Black male's greatest threats and challenges. He is without question a foe. Officer Gung Ho is usually White, young, aggressive, and ready to make a name for himself. Officer Gung Ho can also be Black. He is eager to "knock heads and take names." Race is not as much an issue as opportunity is. When it comes to community-related programs that are proactive in nature, he feels that approach is soft and not real police work. The greatest threat that influences his encounters with Black males is *fear.* He is afraid to get hurt physically as well as socially. He will not be punked. When Officer Gung Ho encounters a young Black man who is muscular and streetwise with an attitude toward police, the outcome is seldom good. The Black man does not want to be punked either. *This is truly a potentially explosive encounter.* A Black man who participates in illegal activity like selling drugs or drunk driving will lose every time. Unpleasant words will be exchanged, and a scuffle may take place. Now Officer Gung Ho has what he wanted in the first place: a reason to make an arrest and use as much force as possible—and then some.

In his own defense, the Black man can only say, "I didn't like the way he stepped to me. He had a nasty attitude." The Black man loses in just about every case. Now there is a personal beef between the two, and other officers are usually introduced into the street battle. Now the Black man has a reputation with other Officer Gung Hos who are expecting and waiting for a confrontation and, more important, for reasonable suspicion to stop.

Cross Police Types

These examples of police types serve as a reminder that there is no such thing as a typical law enforcement officer. They are all different, just like the rest of society, and should not be grouped as one. Understanding this provides the Black man with the opportunity to analyze the officer with whom he is dealing and then determine the officer's motive (when time permits). Essential to this theory is that the Black man must allow himself time to size the officer up. For encounters with local law enforcement, this means seeking to get to know those who patrol one's neighborhood. It may not be uncommon for an officer to be a mix of police types.

Civilians must remember that law enforcement officers are representative of society at large. *They are not a special class of people with badges and authority.* Whatever type of person is in the community, to an extent, we can expect to see this type with a badge. This is the greatest thing forgotten about police. They are the average people in society, with all of the baggage that might come from their experiences in the community. Education and experience usually result in mixed types. For example, imagine having an Officer Gung Ho and an Officer Klan all in one. Watch out! Or imagine an Officer Bill and an Officer Political. This person can run for office and be successful, but he is often a threat to some in upper police administration.

Many young Black officers begin as a cross between Officer Brother and Officer Gung Ho. He is a genuine Officer Brother who has the preconceived perceptions of who the police are combined with pressure from trying to impress his gung ho peers. As he becomes more secure in his job and gains an understanding of all of the dynamics, he usually moves back over to being Officer Brother.

These police types usually work best with local law enforcement where Black men have the opportunity to develop a relationship with the officers. It is more challenging to develop personal relationships with state- and federal-level law enforcement officers. Hopefully, there is less contact with them in any case. Black men must truly be aware of the art of manipulation that often comes from local-level investigators and state- and federal-level law enforcement officers who are also usually investigators of some sort. Their main role or goal is often to gain trust while seeking information, with the intent of gaining enough probable cause for an arrest.

This is where the presence of an attorney is always best. I do not provide this information to interfere with legitimate investigations and interviews necessary to bring the criminal off the street. We must never get away from the fact that some Black men do wrong and need to come off the street and pay the price for their crimes. After all, it is often an issue of Black-on-Black crime. Once again, more Black mentors can help reduce Black-on-Black crime.

Any seasoned and ethical investigator possesses the skills to appropriately use all of the legitimate tools and practices to interview and interrogate in order to determine levels of guilt and innocence. These law enforcement officers should be supported and encouraged to use the appropriate techniques with Black men. Black men simply need to be aware of what is going on. And if the Black man is in the wrong, he needs to speak to an attorney and do the right thing.

Clearly the police typology just discussed is not absolute and does not list all the different police types. The purpose is to understand that not all police can be put into one category. Civilians and police alike should take time to understand with whom they are dealing. They should understand who may be friend or foe and the implications of their own attitudes and actions when they encounter any law enforcement officer.

Just as it is important that Black men understand the diversity of law enforcement officers, it is important for law enforcement officers to understand the enormous diversity among African American men. This is important for several reasons: one cannot prejudge a Black man based on how he looks, his economic status, his education, or where he lives. Many Black men can serve as a resource to law enforcement if law enforcement officers, especially White ones, stop and seek to understand the diversity that exists. If there truly is a discussion from the top down, there is a potential that the patrol-level officer may first seek to get more insight into who they are encountering and maybe even have less fear and fewer assumptions in some cases. There is additional insight that may come from White officers reading this section: many Black men are similar to White men. The following descriptions are discussed in *Destiny Fulfilled: A Black Man's Prevention and Survival Guide to Police Encounters* (Herring, 2016, pp. 19–31).

Black Male Typologies

Just as there are many different types of law enforcement officers, there are many different types of Black men. Black men can also be broadly categorized for the purpose of insight and understanding of their diversity. This is important as officers reflect on who they are or how they may be perceived. This can also play a role in how they determine with whom they associate or from whom they seek advice. A Black man who does not seek counsel and advice from another Black man is truly at a disadvantage. We often tend to hang with our own and seek counsel from those similar to us. This is usually a major mistake. As an example, how many educated Black males in higher-income brackets—who live in upscale communities—seek out men who live in public housing? We should seek to learn from those who see the world from a different perspective, or may need a hand up. That does not necessarily mean taking the advice given; it simply means that there is more information with which to make decisions.

Here are extremely important points of consideration for the law enforcement managers, city and county government administrators, and elected officials who may read this to consider:

1. What do you specifically know about the diversity of the African American men in the community you serve? Take the time to truly write it down for reflection.
2. How much do you socialize with African American men in your community when not working?

3. What are the specific different views that African American men have of law enforcement in your community, and how do you know those are their views?

4. As you read the different typologies, can you identify specific men that may serve as a resource to assist with collaborating with those in the community that may have distrust and anger toward law enforcement?

5. Who do you specifically know that would be willing to assist with implementing programs that foster strengthening law enforcement–Black community relationships while strengthening the resiliency of the community through crime control?

6. And finally, what community resources can you identify for those in need, and how accessible are those resources—as an example, substance abuse counseling and gang intervention activity?

For some larger agencies, command staff may quickly rely on their busy schedules and say that they count on supervisors for this information. A common theme that you will continue to hear from me is that if law enforcement administration is too busy to have personal relationships with members of their community, they are too busy for the responsibility they are assigned with. The lower the level of the supervisor, the more intimate the knowledge and relationship that supervisor should have with those that they police. Sheriffs are more accustomed to having personal relationships and knowledge because of their dependence on individual votes. As an example, every law enforcement manager should have personal relationships with more than one blue-collar brother who feels comfortable coming to the police department or sheriff's office to discuss concerns. That comfort is fostered by the blue-collar brother occasionally being asked to lunch or to participate in law enforcement initiatives. Please note that the following descriptions that you are about to read were originally intimately written for Black men with the goal of them fostering relationships among each other that will assist with avoiding negative law enforcement encounters.

Blue-Collar Brother

The cornerstone and foundation of most Black men's existence is the blue-collar brother. This is the Black man who is simply hardworking and trying to do the right thing. His education is often limited; maybe he did not even finish high school. He is not a perfect Black man. Perhaps he had some minor encounters with the police. He totally understands the game of life and just wants to do his thing and take care of his own. The blue-collar brother is not a deadbeat dad but occasionally falls behind in child support. He has a family and works hard to take care of his own. He is respected by his lady and his children. The blue-collar brother does not have many police encounters because he is busy hustling in a couple of jobs, if not more. He may occasionally drink and even smoke weed, but he will not waste his hard-earned money. He is in love with his kids and works hard to make sure they have a better life than he had. The older he gets, the milder he gets. He feels as if there is a glass ceiling when it comes to economic advancement and opportunity. At some point, he tried to climb the ladder of success but was knocked down. At times he may have stepped out on his lady, but he realized that the other women were more drama than they were worth. He reads the paper and can have deep, insightful conversations on current events. He is usually not active with community affairs, but many come by to seek his opinion.

Here is the thing to remember about the blue-collar brother: do not mess with him, his family, or his home. Do not make him truly mad. He will shoot you to protect his own. He will not physically fight, but somewhere near him there is a gun or a knife. The blue-collar brother is the one man with whom every Black man should have a relationship.

It is important to gain his trust and seek counseling from him. To the gangbanger (discussed later), he can give advice and inspiration without judging. He is the one who can get the gangbanger a job if he is ever willing to work for the low wages. The gangbanger just has to remember not to sell dope in front of the blue-collar brother's house, try to date his daughter, or mess with his son, who is not a gangbanger. The intellectual brother (discussed later) needs to have a relationship with him to remind himself what it is really all about and to stay rooted. Somehow, even with the limited pay, the blue-collar brother has cash on the side and puts all of his children through college.

Buppie

The buppie is a spinoff of the yuppie (young upwardly mobile professional). Yuppies were White, college educated, and in their twenties and thirties. When I think of buppies, I think of Atlanta during the late '70s and early '80s. It seems that if you had a business-related degree and were from the South, you headed to Atlanta and had success. Buppies are the Black upwardly mobile professionals. These Black men have had some success and sometimes get caught up in thinking that they have *really* made it. They make six figures, and their challenge is often keeping up with the Joneses. The nice cars and homes have price tags. They are often politically involved. Their greatest shortcoming is focusing more on the next career move and not enough on the community that produced them. They are to be commended for their success, but sometimes they have to experience reality checks that come in the form of some type of crisis. They often will not reach out to assist other Black men if it means risking their status quo or livelihoods.

Intellectual Brother

The confirmed intellectual brother is the Black man with the serious degrees and knowledge that have proved who he is in a formal setting. There are hundreds of intellectual brothers in America today who work in the theological, scientific, social, political, medical, and business arenas. We often do not give credit to the intellectual brothers for what they experience, endure, achieve, and contribute. They represent what is possible and how far we have come. They often challenge the societal ills that plague Black men. Unfortunately, some Black men often dismiss the intellectual brother, accusing him of not understanding what "real brothers" encounter. This is far from the truth. Intellectual brothers have often been victimized by the system or police during their early years and maybe even in later years. The intellectual brother can provide a dynamic voice for our cause and can bring understanding to those who want to discredit or who do not understand today's Black man's experience with or perception of the criminal justice system.

Unfortunately, it is true that the intellectual brother can get so caught up in his own racial battles and ambition that he loses touch with other Black men. It is up to all of us to support the intellectual brothers and keep them focused. If you do not personally know a few intellectual brothers, the question is "why?"

In addition to the *confirmed* intellectual brother, you have the *unconfirmed* intellectual brother. This is the intellectual brother with a pretty strong IQ who is well read and articulate. He knows his area of expertise. The problem is that he is not documented. With whom do you want to take your chances—someone who read up on surgery or the surgeon who has been to medical school? If you need to go to court, do you trust someone who has read many law journals and law books or a law school graduate? When your new computerized Lexus needs work, do you take it to the self-taught mechanic or the one who is Lexus certified? The unconfirmed intellectual brother has much to offer his community and society. But for these contributions to come to fruition, he is often best crossed with the entrepreneur brother or the social-activist brother. Our community needs the intellect to be utilized.

The intellectual brother can bring legitimacy and respect to the Black man's cause when challenging the criminal justice system. The intellectual brother is heard at different levels in society. But how much is he willing to push to fix the problems in the criminal justice system? That is the question. The unfortunate reality is that even with all of the intellectual brothers out there, the problems in the criminal justice system still exist.

Social-Activist Brother

Thank God for the social-activist brother. He was born with a cause and picks up the slack of many others. He fills a void that must be filled. There have been many—yet few—who truly put the cause before themselves, and often, their families. The social-activist brother is not appreciated until an event brings his plight to the forefront.

Social-activist brothers often have sacrificed much and have had much impact long before they are known at a broader public level. Somehow they understand the broad and deep dynamics of society and humans. Marcus Garvey is an example of a social-activist brother. W. E. B. DuBois is an example of a social-activist brother crossed with an intellectual brother. One of the more popular social-activist brothers who was crossed with the intellectual brother and the spiritual brother was—you got it right—the Reverend Dr. Martin Luther King Jr. Another trifecta brother changing the world and standing up for all Black men through social activism, intellect, and spirituality was Malcolm X.

Recreational User Brother

The recreational user brother works hard, is committed to family, and stays out of trouble. He sees no harm in spending his money as he wishes at the end of the day or week of hard work. He feels that smoking a little marijuana and having an evening or weekend drink does not harm anyone. In criminology, some see this as a victimless crime, but the Black man often does not even see it as a crime. He does not see himself as addicted and is rather offended if you refer to him as addicted. The reality *often* is that he is addicted, but you will not convince him of this. Internally, he knows he participates in these activities to escape some level of unhappiness at home or dissatisfaction with life in general. He does not realize the harm or danger that he introduces to his family by purchasing illegal weed or by occasionally driving drunk. To him, it is not drunk driving since he is rather functional when he drinks. He believes his body has developed a high tolerance.

The weed smoker must get his weed from somewhere. He does not realize that every time he purchases it, he puts his family and career at risk. The longer he goes without an incident, the more immune he feels. The weed smoker is exposing his family to the criminal element and law enforcement. More people know about his illegal smoking activity than he thinks. His kids know he smokes, and often they also smoke—whether openly or in the closet. The downfall of the recreational weed smoker may be one of the following:

1. He fails a urine test at work.
2. He does not get a promotion or cannot apply for another job because he did not pass the urine test.
3. He gets caught up in a small raid as the result of a drug investigation. The charge is minor, but now his business is public.
4. His kids join his theory on recreational use but are not as mature as him. Their recreational habits lead them to more serious drug use and involvement with a bad crowd.
5. He is at the wrong place at the wrong time; this includes maybe a traffic checkpoint or a police response to his house. His small stash is found. He now has a simple possession charge.

6. The marijuana use serves as a gateway to another drug. That is, the marijuana use seduces him into trying another recreational drug, sometimes crack.

There is no such thing as recreational crack cocaine use. Many blue-collar and professional brothers have lost everything by just experimenting with crack or powdered cocaine. I have never heard any of them say, "I saw it coming" or "I thought it could happen." Here is the question for the recreational smoker brother. If not addicted, why risk it? There is no way to justify breaking the law while participating in the illegal activity.

The recreational drinker is more of a risk in some ways than the recreational smoker. This is because buying alcohol is legal. There is sometimes a fine line between the recreational drinker and the hardcore alcoholic. The transition is often slow. We sometimes get caught up in saying that there is a difference between the individual who sips cognac from a cute glass and the drunk brother on the street who drinks the cheapest and hardest thing he can get. The bottom line is that it's all alcohol, and it's all addictive. The greatest challenge and loss to the recreational drinker is the time wasted during a light high. He is willing to sacrifice quality time for the high time. He is missing quality time with family or the community. He has much to offer the community, and his absences during high times add up. The downfall of the drinking brother may include the following:

1. There is a guaranteed shortness of life due to the effects of alcohol on the liver.
2. He may incur a DUI and all of the associated costs.
3. The DUI may involve injury to self or someone else and the physical, financial, and emotional costs along with associated jail time.
4. The more you drink as a recreational drinker, the more you drink.

The best hope for the recreational user brother is the spiritual brother. He is not there to convert him but is there to be a friend and eventually strengthen his faith and involvement. Critical health incidents and legal complications are the next motivators of change. Regular physical activity and aggressively engaging in the pursuit of life dreams and goals can mitigate negative impacts.

Community Brother

The community brother is different from the social-activist brother. He is not committed to bringing change; he is just committed to being there and making his neighborhood livable. He does not seek attention and does not want to be in the spotlight. He is involved in grassroots change in the neighborhood. He works with organizations like the Boy Scouts and the Boys and Girls Clubs of America. He coaches sports teams and is truly committed. There are fewer and fewer community brothers due to the economy and the necessity for his type to work more hours and jobs. Many local organizations and governments make it more difficult for him to provide leadership due to regulations and reduction of funds. I am willing to bet that research would show that as community brothers' presence declined, gangs increased. It has become difficult to identify community brothers. It seems that these men are all just too busy. We have become more of a society that looks out for and takes care of only immediate family.

Entrepreneur Brother

The entrepreneur brother is the Black man who refuses to work for someone else and always has a private venture going. There are different levels of success for entrepreneur brothers. True entrepreneur brothers totally relieve themselves of working for someone else and are successful at what they do. They are highly motivated, incredibly self-confident, and motivated or driven by money. Those who are successful often give back to the community. Check this out—imagine the entrepreneur brother joining forces with the community brother. Now you've got something. Entrepreneur brothers have the potential to bring significant change to the Black community.

When it comes to relationships with police, the greatest challenge for the entrepreneur brother is to never become so impatient that he is willing to try to take shortcuts to gain success. He must always stay in legitimate business.

Gangbanger Brother

The gangbanger brother is the one who is involved in gang life. This is probably one of the fastest-growing populations of Black men over the past couple of decades. They are now present even in small and rural communities. Maybe the spiritual brothers need to study them and see why gang organizations have been so successful in recruiting young Black men. But this would involve the spiritual brother leaving the walls of the place of worship and taking to the streets.

Gangbangers join gangs for different reasons: greed, security, love, and most damning of all, the feeling that there are no other options. There are different levels of gangbanger brothers. Some will do anything to rise up in the ranks and have given up on relationships outside of the organization; others find themselves in by circumstance. Black men must try to reach those who find themselves in by circumstance before their involvement and commitment grow. Most gangbangers age out, and many would get out if there were options. Gangbanging often begins with a sense of hopelessness. We know this and do not need research to tell us about our own, yet we still struggle with intervention.

The gangbanger brothers have the most violent relationships with police. They do not trust the police, and the police do not trust them. There are, of course, all levels of crime associated with gangbanging. The best way to reach a gangbanger is through a personal relationship with a police brother, spiritual brother, community brother, or blue-collar brother. Unfortunately, Black men are often too busy or too afraid to help guide a gangbanger out. Most gangbangers end up in jail, injured, or dead. By the time they age out, if they make it, options are limited. Gangbangers who age out and become one of the other positive influences on Black men have an opportunity to reach current gangbangers, changing and potentially saving their lives. We can never give up on any Black man, period.

Street Crimes Brother

The street crimes brother makes a living from illegal activity. He makes his living getting over on others in the Black community. He may sell drugs, steal cars, or participate in burglaries. The street crimes brother believes that the only way he can get what he believes is his is to do it illegally. He has no confidence in society's ways of making a living. He often believes that the White man will not allow the Black man to make it. Some street crimes brothers are violent, and some are not. They are individualists and have no interest in becoming a gangbanger brother. Street crimes brothers have been in and out of the criminal justice system and are well educated about the system. They are not at all afraid of the police, and they know how police operate. Police are familiar with them and their modus operandi. They are the first ones who come up in police discussions when a crime has been committed.

Sex Addict Brother

The sex addict brother is the Black man whose sex drive guides his life choices. There are different levels and different types. There are the perverts who prey on young children by winning their trust. There are the quasi-perverts who prey on teenagers of legal age. There are the violent rapists who forcibly violate anyone—young or old, male or female. There are the sex addict brothers who do not use any self-control and must have sex with several women. What is interesting is that some of the women they date are aware of them having sex with numerous other women.

The sex addict brother often does not realize that he has an addiction. When the urge strikes, he must fulfill his desire. He is not concerned with spreading disease or causing pregnancy. He often has violent encounters with the boyfriends and husbands of the women with whom he is having sex.

There are also sex addict sisters and women who allow sex addict brothers to do their thing. A major fault of some responsible Black men is that they do not have candid, open, preventive, educational conversations with younger Black men about the power of their sex drives, how to control their sex drives, and the lure of the sex addict sister.

Used-to-Be-Black Brother
The used-to-be-Black brother is the Black man who associates himself with Whites more than Blacks. While he may blame it on economics, politics, or women, he has a psychological issue about Blacks. I do not mean the Black man who dates, marries, or associates outside of his race. I mean the Black man who looks down on other Black men and overall has turned on—or away from—them.

The Teenage Brother
It is imperative to acknowledge and separately identify those young Black men who are going through their teenage years—those Black men who are in

search of manhood while figuring out what being a man is about. Some of these young Black men can go to war, yet they cannot legally drink in most states. Some of these young Black men cannot only vote, but their collective numbers can make the final decision, and they are *not* aware of their political power. They see the power, riches, and fame of living in the strongest country in the world, yet often they feel that the world is against them. They have a natural sexual drive that often becomes the primary force in life. They can be and will be directed by someone or something, and this has always been the case.

The teenage brother has been labeled, blamed, and targeted while deciding that he must take his life into his own hands. He is in search of manhood, but he is often still living in childhood. In many cases, he has been pampered and spoiled by his mother and expects to get his way. Other Black men have proved time after time that they do not have time for him. They come into his life at a time of crisis and convenience only to retreat until the next opportunity. The teenage brother will seek acceptance and support somewhere. Often that support appears to have genuine interest and love, but it may also be a gang, a church, a sports team, a big brother, a drug dealer, a group of friends, or unfortunately, a sexual predator. The teenage brother has been told—by his father, mother, uncle, friends, favorite music artists, and media—that the police are the enemy.

Spiritual Brother

I have saved for last the type of man I think is the most important resource to all Black men—the genuine spiritual brother. There are a lot of self-serving brothers out there who may call themselves spiritual brothers. The spiritual brother is committed to his faith and believes that his faith is the answer to all of the problems of the world and specifically the plight of Black men. The challenge of understanding and communicating with the spiritual brother involves knowing who is real. Unfortunately, there are many self-proclaimed spiritual brothers who are primarily interested in using association with their religions for their personal advantage. It is really all about them. Some may even hold positions of authority and respect in their religious groups and communities. They cause more harm than the crack addicts who steal, because people trust them. Black men must not worry about the self-serving, corrupt, false prophets. Their hypocrisy will be taken care of at a much higher level.

As a follower of Jesus the Christ, I know that the focus should be on coming to the aid of others before oneself. One thing that has always impressed me about my Muslim brothers is their discipline.

Every time I see a Nation of Islam brother who was hardcore hood but is now selling *The Final Call* newspaper and bean pies in the street in a suit on a hot day, I say, "Wow!"

About ten years ago, I became associated with some in the Bahá'í faith. This is one of the most multiracial, welcoming faith organizations, in the community, and in the world, to which I have ever been introduced.

There are numerous others, of course, but those associated with American Black men are limited. The spiritual brother at one time was the leader in addressing issues that affected the Black community. It is obvious that somewhere along the way, something happened. All we have to do is look at growth in the gang community.

The genuine spiritual brother who is committed, available, and willing to put others before himself is still the best hope for our community. For me, that means accepting Jesus as Savior and not being afraid of submitting to the leadership of the Holy Spirit and the leadership placed before me. Every brother needs a close, personal relationship with a spiritual brother.

Significance of Brother Types

Understanding the significance of brother types is very important. First, the types allow Black men to slow down and reflect on who they are. This is especially important for the younger Black men who have not had the opportunity to realize that they have much potential and that many of their contributions could strengthen society. These young Black men must first begin to have some positive insight into their own value and worth. If you have been told what and who you *are not* most of your life, it is difficult to see who you *are.*

If you are too busy hustling to survive after getting caught up in the game, it is difficult to feel the gold within you. If you are that hardworking blue-collar brother who has focused on working two and three jobs to take care of your family, you are often too tired to realize the gold within you that influences so many others.

First, who do you say you are? Take a look at these brother types. Reflect on what is in your heart and who you want to be. Do not worry about whatever game you are caught up in now. Think about your dreams and what would bring you joy. Every gangbanger brother is first someone else. He turns to gangbanging as a lifestyle of survival. He cannot allow his other gangbanger brothers to know who he really is because it may seem like a sign of weakness. He may even hide his true identity from himself. He does this to reduce the hurt and frustration of feeling that he will never realize his dreams.

And who is responsible for his not realizing his dream and the dreams of other Black men he knows? In his mind, the police will take away even more opportunities and freedom. The police can easily become the face of the enemy.

Understanding your brother type allows you to understand yourself at another level. The more you understand yourself, the more control you have during police encounters. Understanding brother types also allows you to assess the people with whom you associate and strengthens your ability to find other brother types who provide you with the opportunity to support your search to find the gold within you. The more you know about who you are and what your potential is, the less you stress when you encounter police. But what about those teenage years, that critical period of life when you are discovering who you are?

Just as the typologies of law enforcement officers are not all-inclusive, the aforementioned typology of Black men is not all-inclusive. The intent of providing this list from a book written for mothers, fathers, other family members, and mentors to share with those young Black men whom they love, have raised, or have taken under their wings is to bring insight about the diversity of Black men to public sector managers for those whom they serve. Law enforcement managers, public administrators, and elected officials at the highest level who are challenged with the intense and complex dynamics of local government management must seek to better understand and appreciate the Black community they serve and especially Black men, who are so disproportionately arrested and imprisoned. If the policy makers develop the compassion to seek to understand this historic phenomenon of often antagonistic African American–law enforcement relationships, there are hopes that they will develop those policies and programs that can bring about the desperately needed change. It is also hoped and believed that if those at the top set the tone and standard, a culture will develop that envelopes all of those who directly work with neighborhoods on a daily basis. Successful engagement of the African American community relies on a more in-depth understanding of the Black community being served.

3

African American Community Engagement

SIMPLY PUT, ALL community cultures are not the same, and it takes time and effort to learn them, appreciate them, and develop strategies to engage them beyond police–community relations and crime prevention. Many law enforcement administrators do not believe it is their responsibility to invest significant effort into understanding the diverse cultures in their community. Many often think that all they have to do is be equable law enforcement managers. This is one reason so many cities have burned via riots and so many officers at the patrol level develop their own less-than-favorable attitudes toward some minority communities.

In some communities, there are gay cultures, Laotian cultures, White cultures, or Muslim cultures that must be learned about and engaged. There has been apathy among many law enforcement managers that prevented them from taking the time to identify, seek to understand, and strategically engage those cultures that they are mandated to police.

While serving as the support services director for police and fire departments in Decatur, Illinois, I became close friends with the late Lt. Roger Walker of the Macon County Sheriff's Department. His extended family adopted me as one of theirs. This was in the early '90s. Roger went on to become the first Black sheriff in Illinois history in 1998 and was then reelected before the governor appointed him secretary of corrections. What is interesting is that Macon County is approximately 17 percent Black and 76 percent White. To get and keep his job as sheriff, he had to learn about the diverse White cultures of Macon County and did an outstanding job of engaging them. Unfortunately, many police managers who are hired by city managers are not as aggressive in personally learning about those whom they serve. For those who say they are, what if their jobs counted on an election that depended on the minority community? I have been simply amazed at the number of White police chiefs and sheriffs who choose not to acknowledge the uniqueness of the African American communities that they serve and the need to learn about and strategically engage them, prior to a critical incident.

The African American community is unique in the United States due to the historical oppression experienced. That statement alone may challenge some, and that is why there is an extreme level of distrust and hatred among many African American communities toward law enforcement that results in protests and riots. This resistance among many White chiefs and sheriffs to acknowledge what they do not know and understand about the African American community has resulted in some line officers developing negative and aggressive attitudes toward the community. Some Black chiefs have not learned how to garner support from their own staff that could bring about changes in officers' attitudes at the patrol level. Just as important, the staggering, disproportionate amount of crime in many African American communities confirms the lack of understanding of what it takes to police the African American community, controlling crime and improving the quality of life. For those who may disagree and are charged with policing significant African American populations, what stories do the crime statistics and public opinion surveys tell in your communities?

The first part of this book focuses on the organizational assessment that should take place in preparation for strategically engaging the African

American community. The forth chapter focuses on whole-community strategic planning to reduce crime. This chapter focuses on engaging the African American community. Like many communities, the Black community has extremely diverse interests. These interests includes economics, politics, and faith, to name a few. There is absolutely no one voice, yet many agree on the challenges when it comes to crime and quality of life. Law enforcement managers and local government managers must be cautious about accepting one or two voices as a total representation of the Black community. This chapter provides a very brief discussion of select organizations that can be engaged for strengthening relationships with the African American community. This limited selection of organizations includes the following:

- public housing
- faith community
- Masonic community
- historically Black colleges and universities
- businesses
- fraternities and sororities

Public Housing Residential Councils

There are public housing communities in most US cities, small and large, and many rural communities now have them as well. According to the US Department of Housing and Urban Development (HUD), there are approximately 1.2 million households living in public housing units, managed by some 3,300 housing authorities (Housing and Urban Development, "HUD's Public Housing Program," n.d.).

According to the HUD Resident Characteristics Report, the following national statistics reflect the population in these housing units:

Race/Ethnicity

- White: 50 percent
- Black: 45 percent
- Hispanic or Latino: 25 percent
- Non-Hispanic, or Latino: 75 percent

Income

- average annual income: $14,455
- extremely low income category (below 30 percent of median): 65 percent or 611,942 residents
- very low income category (below 50 percent of median): 21 percent or 194,610 residents

Length of stay

- five to ten years: 19 percent
- ten to twenty years: 17 percent
- over twenty years: 13 percent

(Housing and Urban and Development, "Resident Characteristics Report," n.d.)

It may be surprising to some that the majority of HUD residents are White (50 percent). The alarming issue with the 45 percent Black resident statistic is that the Black population makes up an estimated 13 percent of the US population. If all things were equal, the Black population in public housing would be 13 percent, yet it is more than triple that amount. These disproportionate statistics are also present in incarceration rates for Black men as well as juvenile-delinquency adjudication rates. The income statistics tell us what we already know: our nation's poorest and most vulnerable live in public housing. Research tells us that there is a relationship between poverty and crime. The third category, length of stay, tells us that 49 percent of the residents stay more than five years, and more than 30 percent stay more than ten years.

Law enforcement agencies police and engage with public housing properties differently. In some communities, public housing has its own law enforcement. In others, local law enforcement assigns patrol officers to work in public housing communities. And in some other communities, the patrol districts are responsible for the public housing communities in the district. The level of engagement between public housing communities and local law enforcement vary. Often, communities have well-established resident councils that meet on a monthly basis. Many law enforcement agencies have representatives who attend monthly meetings, but seldom are measurable goals set while engaging other social-service agencies. Public housing communities provide a great opportunity to engage a portion of the African American community to develop relationships, but more than monthly meetings are needed, and command staff should periodically get involved or review reports of progress. As the police chief in Hartsville, South Carolina, and Salisbury, North Carolina, I would often participate in foot patrols in the public housing communities. As previously mentioned, in Salisbury, I moved my family into public housing for about a year. My greatest surprise came from those officers that expressed their surprise and thought I was putting my family in danger. I thought, these are the communities that you are challenged to make safe. How hard would you work to make things safer if you lived there? This made me think about something that you do not see much nationally anymore, officers who were raised in the communities that they police and still live in those same neighborhoods.

There seems to be great disrespect toward public housing residents and communities from many in public safety. Considering the poverty, crime, and youth/senior vulnerability, how much attention is given to the communities beyond crime control? As an example, while it has probably taken place some-where, I have never heard of tabletop exercises in preparation for natural disasters or active shooters in public housing communities. As the executive director of the Institute for Homeland Security and Workforce Development at North Carolina Central University, I have led my staff in collaborating with Durham Housing Authority to assess and develop more thorough emergency operation plans. It has been a long, slow, tedious process to find external funding for this comprehensive planning.

Faith Community
The faith community can serve as an excellent source to engage the Black community. Some law enforce-ment agencies have done an outstanding job of devel-oping relationships with their local faith community. Many faith organizations would be glad to collaborate with local law enforcement but must be educated on opportunities. Law enforcement administrators must become familiar with the diverse faiths in their com-munities. In collaboration with the Rural Domestic Preparedness Consortium and the Federal Emergency Management Agency, the Institute for Homeland Security and Workforce Development (IHSWD) cre-ated MGT 405, "Mobilizing Faith-Based Communities in Preparing for Disaster." This eight-hour work-shop has been facilitated in more than forty com-munities throughout the United States. Through the

development and delivery of the course, I became even more impressed with the diversity of faith organizations throughout the United States and the services they proudly, efficiently, and effectively bring to their communities and others throughout the nation and beyond.

The Black community is widely represented in a number of faiths. As I mentioned in the Black male typologies previously discussed, I have always been impressed with the Islamic community when I would see certain Black males on the corner selling bean pies and *The Final Call* newspaper. On several occasions, I have seen young men on those corners who I knew were previously heavily engaged in illegal activity. I often thought, "Wow!" Due to the outreach, their Muslim Brothers had not only converted them, but they now had the discipline that would allow them to stand in the heat on street corners. That took the willingness to go after them and show them another option for living. The point for the emphasis once again? I wonder how many law enforcement organizations beyond large urban ones, strategically engage the Muslim community.

In 2008 the IHSWD sponsored a colloquium in collaboration with the Army War College (www. strategicstudiesinstitute.army.mil). *Opportunities for Engaging Minority Communities in Securing Our Nation*

(Owens, 2008). Key insights from the entire colloquium from the Army War College website are as
follows:

- Successful engagement of minority communities by community, state, and national security agencies requires cultural understanding
and appreciation for diversity within and
among the agencies and willingness by agency
leaders to initiate contact, either directly or
through mutually trusted agents.
- Understanding generational differences within
minority communities is important for successful engagement, especially for long-established
communities that continue to receive new
members from foreign locations.
- Security agencies must have the ability to
communicate effectively with minority communities to establish mutual trust and successfully engage their members.
- Disadvantaged and at-risk communities, with
or without minority populations, are especially vulnerable to disasters and require
particular attention when planning for miti-
gation, response, and recovery.
- There is a long and honorable tradition of
service by minorities in securing their nation;
that service must continue to be recognized

as the basis for continued participation and leadership by minority members.

Among the many presentations, one included a panel discussion with North Carolina law enforcement representation from Charlotte, Salisbury, and Durham, to name a few. In addition, a panel of local Imams participated in a discussion. I remember one of the head Imams from the Research Triangle area beginning with a comment something to the effect of, "It is about time that someone asked us about keeping our community safe." The following is a select comment about their presentation per the Army War College website: "Four Imams, representing two North Carolina Muslim communities, assessed their constituents' relationship to security organizations. They recommended methods to successfully engage their constituents to enhance participation in planning for and responding to natural disasters and terrorism threats. The Imams emphasized trust and successful communications, as well as the need for understanding cultural diversity within Muslim communities."

Considering the climate after the events of 9/11, it would behoove many local law enforcement communities to strengthen relationships with their Islamic communities. Those relationships may prove to be beneficial on many levels. Time should be taken to learn and respect the culture. Some of the largest law enforcement organizations have dedicated units for collaboration.

While Chief in Hartsville, South Carolina, I developed relationships with members of the Bahá'í faith. Over the years, I have found Bahá'í to be one of the most diverse faiths emphasizing unity. In Hartsville, Bahá'í members were very active with our police-community strategy meetings and offered diversity training for the police department.

Some of the information in the following section about the Christian community and other faith organizations engagement with law enforcement is from my doctorate of ministry dissertation that was converted into a book, *African American Men and the Police: A Christ Solution for the New Millennium* (Herring, 2015).

Churches and Black Community–Law Enforcement Engagement

In *The Role of African-American Churches in Reducing Crime among Black Youth,* Byron Johnson examined how religious involvement of African American youth significantly shields them from the effects of neighborhood disorder and the decay of youth crime. Researchers have documented that the African American church has been an important agency of social control and organization among Black Americans, and yet its potential influence for promoting pro-social behavior among Black Americans has been largely ignored by criminologists (Herring, 2015).

While some local law enforcement organizations collaborate with predominately Black churches, it is often after a critical incident or, for sheriff's offices, during election time. Seldom have I witnessed, or heard of local law enforcement proactively and strategically engaging the Black church to reduce crime by addressing the needs of at-risk youth in the community. Many churches have programs that engage their youth, but not in collaboration with local law enforcement. All too often local law enforcement administration is too busy, or feels it is not their role to engage in such proactive collaboration that to some may seem more social than policing. That is until there are critical incidents like shootings and riots.

I recall hosting a round table discussion at a church in Durham, North Carolina, with local law enforcement and a church men's ministry. While four of the six law enforcement agencies invited attended, one large law enforcement agency replied that they could not force officers to participate in religious functions. Two years later, in that same city, there was an officer involved shooting of a Black male. After protests in the city, that law enforcement agency was holding meetings with local clergy.

Johnson's research went beyond law enforcement and church collaboration, it explored whether church involvement diminishes the harmful effects of neighborhood decay and whether by such diminishment, Black youth involvement in the church helps control criminal behavior (Herring, 2015). But here is an interesting point: What does the Black youth hear and experience in the church? I have encountered pastors who have an extreme distrust and even anger toward police and even express this from the pulpit. While defending my dissertation for my doctor of ministry degree, the dean of the doctor of ministry program who was present during my predefense, became agitated to the extent of raising his voice and pointing his finger. He was upset that my research and intervention focused on Christian men bringing about change and did not more adequately address police bringing about change. Due to his experiences with police during his youth, he considered police dishonest and abusive. I had experienced the frustration with police relationships and the Black community on a number of occasions. What was scheduled as a fifteen-minute predefense overview turned into a two-hour attack about why my project did not focus more on what law enforcement should do. The following day I met with him for approximately two hours. I discussed my proactive efforts as a police chief to strengthen Black community relationships, my experience with the Commission of Accreditation for Law Enforcement Agencies (CALEA), my work with the US Community Policing Consortium, and my challenges with bringing about law enforcement organizational change. I showed him actual examples of my work from local newspapers. I also shared with him the high levels of organizational backlash that I experienced. I then discussed with him how my research focused on using Christian men to mentor young Black males from a Christian doctrine perspective about engaging law enforcement and bringing about change in the criminal justice system. After that two-hour meeting, he apologized and said he got it and saw how he had been part of the problem.

Here was a veteran pastor, highly respected, active in the community and dean at a theological school who had not experienced law enforcement reaching out to him to the extent of changing his very negative view of law enforcement and the criminal justice system while providing a venue to get engaged in policing the community in which he lived, pastored, and worked. Just think of his influence at his church, at the theological school and in the community. What did the many youth who had come into his presence hear about police?

When considering Johnson's research, is it possible that Black youth involvement in church may not only diminish criminal behavior but also improve perceptions of law enforcement? For this to take place, law enforcement and local government leadership must provide the platform for church leadership to not only proactively communicate with local law enforcement but be shown opportunities to participate in proactive, long-term initiatives that can reduce crime and strengthen relationships between the Black community and law enforcement. The US Department of Justice Office of Community-Oriented Policing Services has made some progress in this area.

The value-based initiative (VBI) was a COPS-funded strategy that emphasized training and technical assistance for problem solving on a grassroots level. Following is a limited selection of the VBI collaboration that focused on strengthening the relationship between police and the faith communities (Herring, 2015, p. 60).

Building a Generation, Redlands, California
This VBI project was from the police chief's Clergy Advisory Council. The council consisted of about ten respected area faith leaders and functioned as a kind of spiritual SWAT team. The members met monthly with

the chief and were also available on an on-call basis as needed.

Ministers against Crime (MAC)

This program was part of the VBI project in Fort Worth, Texas. MAC helped the police keep potentially volatile situations from escalating to violence and conducted nightly crime patrols.

Cops and Clergy Network (CCN)

CCN, a coalition of police, clergy, and other faith-based organization (FBO) leaders, was established in 1998 by a minister who believed that law enforcement officials and people of faith had more in common than they might think. CNN was established in Redlands, CA.

Faith Leaders Ministerial Academies

Faith Leaders Ministerial Academies is a generic name for a police-sponsored training program for clergy and other FBO leaders with the purpose of educating clergy about local law enforcement.

In conclusion, the faith community can serve as an excellent source for engaging the African American community. The faith community is very diverse, and only a few select examples were given; this is not intended to make light of or disrespect any faith not discussed. Law enforcement agencies must identify the organizations within their own communities, seek to learn their cultures, and develop engagement plans. Some sheriffs are known for not engaging the faith community until election time, making those popular church visits. Chaplains are, of course, an excellent resource. Agencies should only utilize certified chaplains.

Masonic Community

This is one of those areas of which I have very little formal knowledge since I am not a Mason. Here is what I do know: in every community in which I have lived and many where I have traveled—large, small, rural, or urban—I met Black men who were Masons. As a police chief, I have seen rings and emblems on cars and buildings that quickly identify them. As one example, Prince Hall Freemasons have a rich history in the African American community and have a church foundation. They are committed to community service, social justice, and the advancement of the Black community. "Prince Hall is recognized as the father of Black Masonry in the United States. Historically, he made it possible for Negroes to be recognized and enjoy all privileges of free and accepted masonry. Today, the Prince Hall fraternity has over 4,500 lodges worldwide, forming forty-four independent jurisdictions with a membership of over 300,000 masons" (Freemason Information, 2016).

My intention is to highlight the outstanding resource that the Masons can serve as when it comes to local law enforcement community engagement. Throughout my nationwide travels while working with law enforcement organizations, seldom have I encountered law enforcement agencies that strategically collaborate with Black Masonic lodges and implement programs to reduce crime and improve the quality of life in the community.

Historically Black Colleges and Universities

HBCUs can serve as an extremely valuable resource for law enforcement agencies when it comes to engagement and collaboration. I have addressed some of this in the organizational assessment and recruitment section of this book. Even if the agency does not have an HBCU in its jurisdiction, it would be more than worth their time and effort to reach out to one, even if in another state. Once again, as a product of one of these institutions (NCCU), I have worked at two (Livingstone College and NCCU) and collaborated with many. HBCUs provide the opportunity for local law enforcement agencies to seek opinions from students via surveys, solicit assistance in conducting local community surveys, recruit employees (civilian and sworn), and facilitate round table discussions and internships. Other than recruitment, many local law enforcement organizations do not take full advantage of this excellent resource. There are 107 HBCUs spread throughout the nation. (White House Initiative on Historically Black Colleges and Universities, n.d.). The US Department of Education houses the White House Initiative on HBCUs.

African American Businesses

Most law enforcement administrators understand the value of developing relationships with the business community. Many may not recognize the historic significance of Black businesses and the respect they garner in the Black community. At one time, Black businesses were the heartbeat of the neighborhood, right behind the church and faith community. This was partially due to Blacks not being allowed to do commerce with White businesses, and when allowed, access was often restricted. This, of course, was more relevant in the midwestern and southern states. At one point in history, the Black business districts thrived—some to historical acclaim, like those in Harlem. In Durham, North Carolina, the North Carolina Mutual Life Insurance Company serves as an excellent historical example. The following information was retrieved from the North Carolina History

Project website (North Carolina History Project, 2016).

During the nadir of race relations in the United States, African Americans had difficulty finding affordable life insurance. African American fraternal orders, such as the Grand United Order of the True Reformers and the Royal Knights of King David, assisted disadvantaged African Americans and provided services to African American communities that might have otherwise been ignored. Inspired by fraternal solutions to societal problems, seven black community leaders started an African American insurance company.

Today, North Carolina Mutual Life (NCML) is the oldest and largest African American life insurance company in the nation. It began in 1898, with the name North Carolina Mutual and Provident Association, and the Durham-based company started doing business in 1899 to relieve "the distress of Negroes." A local barbershop owner, John Merrick, served as the first president. According to historian Loren Schweninger, the association was "primarily responsible for the expansion of the property-holding [blacks] in the area." Property holdings in the city soon surpassed population growth. In a few decades, writes historian Jeffrey Crow, NCML became the "largest black-owned business in the United States" and later influenced the establishment of similar entrepreneurial endeavors, including the Mechanics and Farmers Bank.

Today, the African American business owner is still greatly respected in the Black community, especially those who located their businesses in Black neighborhoods. The diversity is great, including the corner store, the insurance agency, the car dealership, and the funeral home (in many Black communities, funeral home directors have a high degree of respect). Law enforcement administration must learn the dynamics of the African American businesses in their city, and seek to engage them to strengthen relationships with the Black community and for support of needed programs.

Fraternities and Sororities
Black sororities and fraternities have played a significant role in Black communities for a long time. This is another type of organization of which I never took the opportunity to become a part, but

I have collaborated with on a number of occasions. Most universities, Black and White, have Black fraternities and sororities on their campuses that are mandated to participate in community service. As an example, the Los Angeles Police Department has a great resource in the many Black fraternities on their numbered universities and colleges. In addition to campus charters, graduate chapters are in most communities and are also committed to community service. The following information was retrieved from the National Pan-Hellenic Council, Inc. website (2015):

> The National Pan-Hellenic Council, Incorporated (NPHC) is currently composed of nine (9) International Greek letter Sororities and Fraternities: Alpha Kappa Alpha Sorority, Inc.; Alpha Phi Alpha Fraternity, Inc.; Delta Sigma Theta Sorority, Inc.; Zeta Phi Beta Sorority, Inc.; Iota Phi Theta Fraternity, Inc.; Kappa Alpha Psi Fraternity, Inc.; Sigma Gamma Rho Sorority, Inc.; Phi Beta Sigma Fraternity, Inc.; and Omega Psi Phi Fraternity, Inc. NPHC promotes interaction through forums, meetings and other mediums for the exchange of information and engages in cooperative programming and initiatives through various activities and functions.

I am sure many law enforcement organizations with Black employees (civilian and sworn) have employees who are members of Black sororities and fraternities. Considering the many Black Greek members throughout the community, these employees can serve as excellent gatekeepers to engaging those local and state chapters. The Delta Sigma Theta Sorority made disaster and emergency preparedness a priority for a select period of time and has received recognition from the Federal Emergency Management Agency. Their Concord, North Carolina, chapter hosted the MGT 405 workshop, "Mobilizing Faith-Based Communities in Preparing for Disaster" developed by the IHSWD at North Carolina Central University in collaboration with the Rural Domestic Preparedness Consortium.

While the previously mentioned African American organization categories are broad, consisting of multiple organizations within them, there are additional historical organizations that have had significant impacts on the nation in the area of civil rights that could be collaborated with as engagement resources. The NAACP and the National Urban League are two such organizations.

The involvement of these organizations at the community level depends on the specific community, and as previously stated, there are many other organizations that have not been referenced. This section only serves as a guide to encourage public managers to explore the organizations in their local communities.

The point is that there are many opportunities for law enforcement agencies to engage the Black community prior to a negative or critical incident. History has proven that it is much better to take the time to proactively engage the Black community prior to such an event. After a critical event, as time has shown, agencies are often forced into reactively responding to issues of anger, frustration, protests, and riots. Proactive engagement allows the law enforcement agencies to develop relationships with the Black community and can aid in reducing crime and improving the quality of life for the entire community. I have experienced members of the Black community defending the police department at a community meeting when someone was making loud and negative accusations against local police. My staff did not have to defend the police department; the public did it for us. This serves as an example of exactly how it should be, representatives of the Black community coming to the defense of the local police departments and sheriff's offices, calling for patience and confidence in investigations. This can only take place when members of the Black community have an established relationship with law enforcement leadership that was fostered by those law enforcement agencies engaging the Black communities that they serve. A goal of all law enforcement agencies should be to have members of the Black community feel that it is their local law enforcement agency that is committed to improving their quality of life and controlling crime. This is possible; it just takes work.

4

Whole-Community Crime-Reduction Strategic Planning and Community Engagement

THIS IS PROBABLY the most important and challenging part of the book and phase of engaging the African American community to reduce and control crime while improving the quality of life for all citizens, businesses, and visitors. All too often, law enforcement organizations do not know how to systematically engage the whole community to reduce crime or have no interest in seeking out and committing the multiyear resources. All too often the community also does not have the patience or commitment to come together in collaboration, developing long-term (two- to five-year) working groups that will lead to measurable crime-reduction initiatives.

I first learned of the strategy when working in Decatur, Illinois, with Peter Bellmio. I have worked with the process in Knoxville, Tennessee, and started it in Salisbury, North Carolina. While in Decatur, I also had an opportunity to meet and develop a relationship with the late Tim Crowe, one of the leaders in crime prevention through environmental design (CPTED). Tim authored the well-known and respected book with the same name. CPTED provides creative environmental measures that can mitigate illegal drug activity in addition to reducing other criminal acts. A basic Internet search can provide more information about Tim and crime prevention through environmental design. I have worked with elements of strategic crime control in Knoxville, Tennessee; Bowling Green, Kentucky; and Hartford, Connecticut. I have gained more insight about and strengthened my knowledge of components of community engagement strategies from former deputy chief Bill Smith of the San Bernardino, California, Police Department and Ray Galvin of the International Association of Chiefs of Police as mentioned earlier. These experiences and relationships, along with my approximately five years of national training with the US Department of Justice Community Policing Consortium, starting up the North Carolina Center for Community Policing, and nine years of national training as the executive director of the Institute for Homeland Security and

Work Force Development, have made me very confident that this model can reduce crime and improve the quality of life in communities—but only if communities come together and commit their time and resources.

For clarity, the original developers of this model referred to it as a crime-control model and purposely did not say "crime reduction." This was based on the premise that any crime wave can happen at any time, which may result in even a temporal increase in crime, yet the implementation of the model would limit the increase in crime. As a very basic example, imagine that a major residential breaking-and-entering ring caused a spike in the crime rate related to break-ins. With this model engaged, the organization assessed, and the community involved, the suspects might be caught sooner than if all of this were not in place. While the crime rate may have increased 5 percent without the model, it only increased 2 percent with the model. The 2 percent increase is absolutely a success, but it is still not a reduction in crime. The crime increase was controlled. I absolutely support the premise that crime could increase but would be mitigated due to the model. I also know that the crime rate may increase as the community gets more involved and confidence in law enforcement causes citizens to report crimes that in the past they may not have. It is my belief that when studying the longitudinal or long-term effect of the strategy, a reduction of crime will be realized.

When considering the importance of soliciting support and involvement from the whole community at the level needed and the two- to five-year implementation and evaluation process, I am confident that the overall crime reduction will be realized with appropriate analysis, along with a measurable increase in preselected quality-of-life indicators. Once again, it takes commitment from, involvement with, and representation of the whole community.

It has become rather pathetic and all too frequent to witness law enforcement agencies hold community meetings in response to violent crime or other negative public incidents related to police-community relations, with the end result being only the meetings. It is also extremely sad to see organizations and special-interest groups in communities call for meetings and protests to address crime and critical issues, with the end result being that they address the immediate issue at the most. What is often lacking is the community at large coming together to identify crime-related issues (not local law enforcement deciding the solutions) and jointly developing strategies to measurably address crime and quality of life. Often there are many special-interest factions off doing their own things in response to critical issues, and after emotions calm down, people go back to the status quo.

The steps of whole-community crime-reduction strategic planning and community engagement involve a few phases that have already been discussed, along with organizational transformation and establishing strong relationships with segments of the entire community, especially (considering the focus of this book) the African American community. It will take the whole-community approach to truly impact the Black community, and the entire community benefits. Elements of the whole-community crime-reduction strategic-planning phase include the following:

1. selecting the program manager
2. establishing an implementation committee
3. selecting the first communitywide strategy session date
4. marketing the strategy session
5. developing the agenda
6. hosting the strategy session
7. holding follow-up committee meetings

The overarching goal of whole-community crime-reduction strategic planning and community

engagement is to bring together diverse representatives of the entire community; educate them on
law enforcement operations, crime statistics, and
quality-of-life issues; and lead them in collaborative
efforts that result in implementation and evaluation
of specific initiatives that will improve quality of life
while reducing crime.

Selecting the Program Manager

This is one of the most important decisions in the
entire process, determining who will facilitate, or
lead the process for the first two to five years. This
individual or team must have a thorough understanding of the process, including contemporary
law enforcement practices as well as experience
with mobilizing diverse communities. Options
include a position similar to a police planner, a
consultant, a university department, or a tempo-
rary full-time employee. It is imperative to select
someone with knowledge, skills, abilities, and time
to commit to the project. The team or individual
does not need to be familiar with the community,
and it may even be beneficial having someone who
is not familiar with the history and politics or committed to any one faction needing to ask fact-find-
ing questions.

The greatest success that I have seen is when communities contract with an experienced consultant

who should also prepare a team within the community to transition leadership. Even with my experience, when I was police chief of a relatively small community (a transient population of approximately 50,000), I hired a consultant. A university-connected person may bring a team with diverse experience, student resources, and excellent evaluation capabilities. It is possible that the cost of this position and other costs may be supplemented by grants and other forms of external funding from diverse funding sources, including private and non-profit entities.

Establishing an Implementation Committee

After the program manager has been selected, a small strategy-implementation committee needs to be established. The purpose of the committee is to assist the project manager with implementing the first communitywide strategy session. Members of the committee need to be familiar with different aspects of the community, be respected in the community, and have the time and desire to assist. They will be educated once the committee is formed. Potential members of the committee include someone from the law enforcement command staff, someone from city or county government similar to a community planner, a human-relations representative, business-community representation, and Black community representation, along with any other minority group largely represented in the community. The committee will be responsible for assisting with developing the first strategic community meeting agenda; finding a location; assisting with logistics like food, copies, and the like; marketing; sending invitations; and communicating with groups and individuals to confirm their attendance.

Selecting the First Communitywide Strategy Session Date

A lot of thought and consideration must be involved in selecting the first communitywide session dates. Since it is recommended that the first session take place on a Friday evening and continue into the next Saturday, there should be limited conflict with scheduled community events. There are course some faiths that worship on Saturday and this should be taken into consideration. Additional conflicts to consider are high school sports, college sports, religious holidays, large functions, national holiday weekends, local conferences or conventions, and so on. The first session should be scheduled at least three months in advance. It is important to have enough time to market the event and for individuals to plan their schedules yet not make it too far in advance that the marketing has limited impact.

Marketing the Strategy Session

Currently I have in my office a framed full-page ad that was taken out to market the first strategy session in Salisbury, North Carolina. The ad has a large umbrella representing the crime-control model and various elements hanging under the umbrella. Marketing the strategy session should be extensive to illuminate the importance. Avenues that may be used are social media, websites, private media, and invitations to organizations, businesses, and individuals. Creative measures should be explored like giving officers flyers to hand out as they come across people in the community. This act has many benefits including officer engagement. There should be, of course, some form of registration to estimate attendance. Invitations should note that it is important that attendees participate in the full session.

Developing the Agenda

The agenda should be developed based on what works best for the community once the process is understood. One consideration is to hold the session over two days, meeting for two hours on a Friday evening and continuing on Saturday for about six hours. As an example, six thirty to eight thirty on Friday evening and nine to three on Saturday could work. Enough time is needed while taking into consideration what the community may be willing to commit to. Following is a sample of what a Friday evening session may look like:

5:30 p.m.–6:30 p.m.	Registration, light hors d'oeuvres, meet and greet
6:30 p.m.–7:00 p.m.	Welcome and purpose Implementation committee Police chief Sheriff Mayor (city/county) State elected officials Federal elected officials
7:00 p.m.–7:30 p.m.	Overview of agenda/process—program manager
7:30 p.m.–8:00 p.m.	Small group breakouts What would prevent the process from being successful? What questions do you have at this point?
8:00 p.m.–8:30 p.m.	Report out and adjourn until morning

Potential Agenda for Saturday

8:00 a.m.–9:00 a.m.	Sign in, light breakfast, socializing
9:00 a.m.–10:00 a.m.	Overview of law enforcement agency hosting and crime-statistics structure Select programs (complaint system, ride-along, citizen police academy, and the like) Calls-for-service report (by district) Case-closure report Crime-analysis report
10:00 a.m.–10:15 a.m.	Department of Social Services report (poverty, homelessness by race and gender, and similar topics)
10:15 a.m.–10:30 a.m.	Break
10:30 a.m.–10:45 a.m.	Public education report (dropout, literacy, proficiency levels by school, race, and gender)

10:45 a.m.–11:00 a.m. Juvenile-justice report (types/
rates of cases by age, race,
and gender)

***Due to time restraints, handouts with informa-
tion should be provided.***

11:15 a.m.–11: 45 a.m. Small group exercise (three
greatest challenges and
strengths of the community)

11:15 a.m.–12:15 p.m. Small group report out

12:15 p.m.–12:45 p.m. Lunch

12:45 p.m.–1:15 p.m. Small group exercise (three
specific solutions/initiatives
that will strengthen com-
munity resiliency, improve
quality of life, and impact
crime.)

1:15 p.m.–1:45 p.m. Small group report out

1:45 p.m.–2:00 p.m. Break

2:00 p.m.–2:30 p.m. Group selection of top three
or four problems that can

	be addressed by community strengths
2:30 p.m.–2:50 p.m.	Assignment to selected solutions, discussion, exchanging contact information, selection of temporary co-chairs
2:50 p.m.–3:00 p.m.	Closing comments

Hosting the Strategy Session

By now, one should have insight into some of the logistics needed for the first strategy session. I have hosted mine in the cafeteria of a middle school and a meeting room of the public library. It is important to pick a neutral ground for the community. While I have participated in successful sessions at churches for relatively large cities, one must consider the politics and diversity of the local faiths and churches of that community. Discussion about issues like prayer should take place prior, especially considering diverse faiths. One consideration is to provide the opportunity for silent/personal prayer and reflection.

Officers should attend in uniform as well as in plain clothes. It is important that security is taken into consideration but to also show up as a welcoming and partnering presence. This should extend to the parking lot, throughout the session, and until all participants have left. Traditional security measures should not be taken for granted in bathrooms and hallways if a facility like a school is used. Everyone may not be happy about the whole diverse community coming together to address crime and improve the quality of life for all.

The facility should have enough space for breakout rooms or for the small groups to work without disturbing each other. The small groups should have the common guidelines of selecting a recorder to write on easel pad paper and someone to report for the group. Depending on the size of the primary room and number of attendees, microphones at each table may be necessary. Information written on the easel pads should be hung around the room and retrieved by the strategy committee after the meeting to develop notes. The facilitation of the reporting sessions sometimes actually benefits from having someone who is well experienced and not connected to the community. It may become necessary to cut people off, calm them down, and facilitate staying focused on the process. The largest session that I have attended had approximately two hundred people present.

It is also very important for law enforcement leadership to be educated on not being baited into defending policies, practices, and past actions. I recall attending a community meeting with law enforcement command staff in Decatur, Illinois. We spent time prior to the meeting discussing—not responding in a defensive way—but being in listening mode. Considering that this meeting included representatives from the African American community who clearly were not satisfied with the police, I advised them not to use phrases like "you people." I was very proud that a White commanding officer did not respond emotionally as a Black male got in his personal space, raised his voice, and pointed his finger. The White commanding officer clearly won over many in attendance when he did not negatively or defensively respond, although he probably had every right to at some level. He showed a composure that demonstrated professionalism from the top leadership that could serve as an example for all patrol officers.

After things calmed down, he calmly and rather directly responded with something to the effect of, "What you people need to understand…" At that point, many of the Black citizens were commenting, "Who is he calling 'you people'?" A leader in the NAACP is the one who stood up and restored order. This was due to the working relationship between the NAACP and the police department, even though they often did not agree. This leader knew the thoughtful character and heart of the commanding officer due to spending time with him in addressing community concerns. The next morning, during a debriefing among command staff, that commanding officer turned red, looked down, and shook his head, saying, "I know, I know." There was some light laughter from the lesson learned. The comments and laughter were due to my comments to that group prior to the meeting.

Solution and Intervention Examples

Potential solutions and interventions for exploration that have been agreed upon in the past involved issues such as the following:

- juvenile curfews
- gang activity
- minority community confidence in law enforcement
- alarm calls for service
- public transportation stops
- homelessness
- illegal drug sales activity
- citizens police academy
- police athletic league
- victims' advocate unit

These are just a few examples from different communities. Each community will identify and agree upon its own needs. There will be several issues that are identified in the small group discussions. The entire group will be led through facilitation to agree on a select number of issues considering interest, resources, and potential community impact. It is feasible that after the first couple of follow-up meetings, a report will come back to no longer move forward with the solution based on information or data sessions from appropriate organizations that possess the appropriate intelligence on the topic. Inclusiveness is imperative in order to have appropriate input on community issues, problems, and concerns.

Follow-Up Committee Meetings

At the end of the first strategy session, citizens identified and agreed upon three to four interventions or solutions that will improve the quality of life with the potential of reducing crime. The process itself will begin strengthening law enforcement and Black community relations. Some interventions may require a long-term time span when reducing crime, and that is OK. Many of the variables that relate to crime are systemic, and the quick-fix panacea needs to be avoided, relying on the organizations that are mandated to address them. Some of these variables may include literacy, drug rehabilitation, and employment.

It is imperative that follow-up meetings for the entire working group be determined and agreed upon at the first strategy session. Historically, the number of participants will decrease to those who are truly committed and then intermittently slightly increase as the committees begin their work. The lack of participation by some members of the community may actually serve as a defense or motivation for local law enforcement if a critical event takes place—and most likely one eventually will.

As an unfortunate example, I remember a young Black girl being shot by a stray bullet in one of the communities where I was chief. One of the first people to loudly protest and come to my office was someone who was too busy to participate in the community meetings and strategies. After allowing his ranting and raving, I mentioned a few meetings and activities that he chose not to participate in and asked why, noting they had the potential to impact senseless violence in that neighborhood. With not much to say, he lowered his head and mumbled that he should have made time to participate, and then we began to discuss the current critical event. He later became involved in follow-up meetings.

The committee follow-up meetings should occur frequently at first, and then the time span between the meetings may increase to allow committee member work. The objective is to allow time for committees to better understand the issues, develop and implement an intervention, and develop a strategy to evaluate the impact. An established and popular system would be appropriate at this point, such as the SARA model, but there are others that will work. SARA is an acronym for scan, analysis, response, and assessment.

Scan

The committee will gather as much information as possible on the issue. This should include having those most familiar with the problem brief the committee. As an example, if the committee is addressing homelessness, representatives from local shelters and social services may be requested to inform the committee. If the committee is addressing gangs, representatives from the sheriff's office, police department, probation/parole, juvenile court, and the school district may brief the committee. As much information and data as possible should be gathered on the issue.

Analysis

After receiving the briefs/information, the group will then analyze the information. They probably will have picked up a couple of committee members from the scanning sessions. When analyzing the information, the idea is to select a manageable intervention that will mitigate the problem and not necessarily try to eliminate it. Analyzing the information includes finding specifics like frequency, location, time of day, suspects, victims, and so on. As an example, it may be determined that young gang members are being recruited due to not having much to do in a specific section of the community while also joining gangs for protection. One should not underestimate idleness, especially among young African Americans in low-income, single-mother households. While gangs then were not at the level that they are today, my mother made sure that, while growing up in Los Angeles, we were active in sports as much as possible and sacrificed and made time to support us, which was challenging for her as a working mom of three boys of different ages.

Potential manageable solutions for this issue of gang radicalization of young boys in a specific community may include the development or support of a Big Brothers Big Sisters mentoring program. Another solution may be opening or expanding a Boys and Girls Club of America. Another solution may be starting a Police Athletic League program. As previously referenced, I was instrumental in starting a Boys and Girls Club in Hartsville, South Carolina. Though the community was small, we had a growing drug problem and a number of shootings, with a few resulting in death. Even in the small rural community, I had an officer shot in the line of duty. I recall meeting on Saturday mornings with a committee and personally traveling to nearby Florence, South Carolina, to meet with the regional leader for Boys and Girls Clubs of America. While the club did not open until after I left, it is still in operation today.

Once again, these meetings in large metropolitan areas are not attempting to attack large city problems, unless the needed support is truly present. Any large city is in essence a compilation of smaller cities. And, yes, of course the problems cross districts and boundaries. For example, in Los Angeles, this process and solution can be applied to South Central and even then may be isolated to a more specific area since South Central Los Angeles is approximately fifty-one square miles and comprises twenty-five neighborhoods. Or maybe the intervention will take place in my childhood community of Pacoima in the San Fernando Valley of Los Angeles.

Response
The response phase is the implementation phase, and it takes place after a thorough analysis. The response is agreed upon by the entire strategic committee since it may take community and maybe state and federal resources. The response should include a comprehensive project-management program similar to a GANTT chart. This process includes listing tasks, time frames, roles and responsibilities, and needed funding, if any. Potential external funding

opportunities include local tax dollars, private organizations, philanthropic organizations, state grants, and federal grants.

Assessment

The assessment and evaluation phase is extremely important, and often not enough attention is given to it prior to project implementation. This provides an excellent opportunity to collaborate with universities and colleges. The committee will want to measure progress and impact while comparing pre implementation data. It is important to celebrate easily identified successes.

Using the Boys and Girls Club as an example, its' development and completion is one form of evaluation. Youth attendance may be another quantitative measurement. Another variable that may be measured is youth-related crime as well as status offenses—those offenses that only apply to juveniles in the neighborhood. In addition to quantitative evaluation measures, qualitative evaluation measures should be used. Quantitative evaluation measures include statistical data like comparing crime rates. Qualitative evaluation measures include data that may come from interviews and observations. Interviewing the Boys and Girls Club participants at the beginning and end of the first year, as well as their parents, serves as an example.

Once again, the follow-up committee reports to the larger strategic working group will be agreed upon at the end of the first strategic meeting, with the meetings taking place more frequently in the first year. Here is a potential schedule based on the whole-community crime-reduction strategic planning meeting taking place on February 18, 2017:

Whole-Community Crime-Reduction Strategic Planning and Community Follow-Up Meetings Schedule

1st	March 18, 2017
2nd	April 22, 2017
3rd	July 22, 2017
4th	November 11, 2017
5th	March 24, 2018
6th	July 28, 2018
7th	October 20, 2018
8th	January 19, 2019

This schedule serves only as an example, but there are some important considerations. As a reminder, the working groups are meeting in between these dates as needed. While the working groups may communicate using different methods including in person, via Skype, on the phone, and more, the larger committee meetings should take place face-to-face. These meetings are intended for working groups updating the larger committee with collaborative feedback and agreement that may also generate resources. These meetings may be scheduled for only ninety minutes and can take place any evening, day, or weekend. Using a working lunch to generate creativity may also be an option.

The concept is to first let everyone see that the strategic process is long term. Next, more frequent meetings are designed to maintain accountability, motivation, and engagement. A new schedule will be developed at the eighth meeting. This eighth meeting should be an extended meeting to evaluate and begin the process over. This meeting may be scheduled as a six- to eight-hour event similar to the first whole-community crime-reduction strategic-planning and community meeting. These working groups are not intended to be permanent. For instance, the group working on starting a Boys and Girls Club may dissolve in a celebratory fashion on the club's first-year anniversary of operation. These next series of meetings represent a new beginning for the process. All communities change over time and this eighth meeting is very similar to the first, acknowledging that change. Hopefully there are many who have been involved since the first communitywide session, but the reality is that there will be newcomers to the process, as well as the community. Hopefully this eighth meeting represents an end to most goals and the beginning of others as the community commits to continuously assessing community needs and developing initiatives that bring the community together with the mission of controlling crime and improving the quality of life for all citizens, businesses, and visitors.

Conclusion

STRATEGY: A GUIDE to Policing the African American Community is just that—a guide. It is not intended as a perfect resource for strategically engaging the African American community. Rather, it is an educational resource that brings enlightenment, insight, and opportunity. After reading the book, it should be clear that much of the information can be used not only for minority communities but any community. While some will see the recommendations as too intensive, comprehensive, and expensive, or simply shy away from the work, I invite these individuals to reflect more deeply on the dynamics of their Black communities from a crime, quality-of-life, and law enforcement–relationship perspective.

Strategy: A Guide to Policing the African American Community is an attempt to address the issues of Black youths' disproportionate adjudication, Black males' disproportionate incarceration, high dropout rates among Black students, high rates of illiteracy among

Black students, high rates of gang activity in the Black community, and the historically negative relationship between the Black community and law enforcement, all of which have caused many communities to burn. While protests serve as an excellent strategy to bring attention to a social phenomenon, something must take place after the attention is received. *Strategy: A Guide to Policing the African American Community* can be that something.

REFERENCES

Freemason Information (2016). Prince Hall Freemasonry. Retrieved April 3, 2016, from http://freemasoninformation.com/what-is-freemasonry/family-of-freemasonry/prince-hall-freemasonry.

Herring, M. (2015). *African American men and police: A Christ solution for the new millennium.* North Charleston, SC: CreateSpace.

Herring, M. (2016). *Destiny fulfilled: A black man's prevention and survival guide to police encounters.* North Charleston, SC: CreateSpace.

Housing and Urban Development (n.d.). *HUD's public housing program.* Retrieved February 18, 2016, from http://portal.hud.gov/hudportal/HUD?src=/topics/rental_assistance/phprog.

Housing and Urban Development (n.d.). *Resident characteristics report.* Retrieved February 18, 2016, from http://portal.hud.gov/hudportal/HUD?src=/program_offices/public_indian_housing/systems/pic/50058/rcr.

Hughes, F & Andre, L. (2007). Problem officer variables and early warning systems, *The Police Chief*

74, no. 10. Retrieved February 18, 2016 from http://www.policechiefmagazine.org/magazine/ index.cfm?article_id=1313&fuseaction=display.

National Pan-Hellenic Council (2015). *Mission.* Retrieved April 3, 2016 from http://www.nphchq. org/mission/.

North Carolina History Project (2016). *North Carolina Mutual Life.* Retrieved April 3, 2016 from http://northcarolinahistory.org/encyclopedia/ north-carolina-mutual-life/.

Owens, D. (2008). *Opportunity for engaging minority communities in securing our nation.* Retrieved April 3, 2016 from https://strategicstudiesinstitute.army. mil/pubs/display.cfm?pubID=857.

White House Initiative on Historically Black Colleges and Universities (n.d.). *What is an HBCU?* Retrieved April 3, 2016 from http://sites.ed.gov/ whhbcu/one-hundred-and-five-historically-black-colleges-and-universities/.

About the Author

D R. MAULIN CHRIS Herring has dedicated more than three decades of his life to public safety. He serves as the executive director of the Institute for Homeland Security and Workforce Development and teaches as a visiting professor of criminal justice at North Carolina Central University. His dedication to public service includes work as a public safety officer, police sergeant, narcotics officer, support services manager, director of the North Carolina Center for Community Policing, and police chief.

Communities and law enforcement agencies throughout the United States have consulted with Dr. Herring. As a police chief, he implemented programming that focused on how police engage with Black males and organized round tables during which officers and Black men could speak directly. Herring earned graduate degrees in public administration, sociology, and divinity. Dr. Herring regularly speaks to the media as an expert on topics related to terrorism, emergency management, and Black male/police relations.